Riders of the Range

BY THE SAME AUTHOR

Continued Next Week
World of Laughter
Kops and Custards
Bound and Gagged
Clown Princes and Court Jesters (with Sam Gill)
Collecting Classic Films
Winners of the West
Dreams for Sale
Ladies in Distress
Mack Sennett's Keystone
Collecting Vintage Cameras
Glass, Brass & Chrome
Gentlemen to the Rescue

Riders
of The Range

The Sagebrush Heroes
of the Sound Screen

by

Kalton C. Lahue

CASTLE BOOKS – NEW YORK

Library of Congress Cataloging in Publication Data

Lahue, Kalton C.
  Riders of the range.

  1. Moving-picture actors and actresses, American—Biography.
2. Western films. I. Title.
PN1998.A2L32   791.43′028′0922   77-168370

This Edition Published by Arrangement with A. S. Barnes & Co., Inc.

Printed in the United States of America

To
Alice and Bonnie—
with many thanks

Contents

Preface

The immediate and warm reception my *Winners of the West* met with upon its publication has brought forth *Riders of the Range* as a companion volume. Like its predecessor, this is also a quite personal and very subjective account, but one dealing with the program or B western of the talkie era from its beginning in 1930 to its death in 1954. While the opinions and observations on the following pages may not be in accord with the readers' views and recollections, they represent countless hours spent in a darkened theatre years ago and more recently refreshed by many additional hours watching my personal favorites in action once again through the magic of lengthy strips of talking celluloid. To those who look in vain for favored western stars like Tim McCoy, Hoot Gibson, Tom Mix and others whose careers began in the silent era, they will be found in *Winners of the West;* while making the present volume somewhat thinner in size, unnecessary duplication has thus been avoided.

In *Winners of the West,* one of my major criticisms of the silent western was the evil that eventually brought their demise—sound. The talkie western gained the potential of a far more realistic format but the repetition of plotting and story structure prevalent in the silent era continued, which was to be expected. Westerns were ground out of story mills on a clockwork basis; directors often shot the same stories so many times that scripts were actually a bother, and writers proficient in revamping their own work (with or without ingenuity) lived reasonably well from the fruits of one idea.

Sound also brought music to the western genre, and with the

9

introduction of the singing cowboy the essence of reality (and any pretense at such) disappeared from the screen. But this too was to be expected. Almost from the movies' beginning, producers had deliberately aimed their product at the so-called "12-year old mentality" and we ate it up with gusto. Program westerns and serials were a staple diet in small-town America of a few decades ago, and in a depression economy they provided for all pure escapism at its best.

With this in mind, I'm about to introduce the *Riders of the Range*, my final work dealing with the cinema. Some years ago, I put pen to paper with a plan in mind, and with the publication of this volume, the plan is now complete. Along the road, I've met many interesting people and have enjoyed numerous pleasant conversations about our favorites. To all who have become loyal readers of my work, I hope that they have enjoyed the long road as much as I have. To those who have assisted me in my research and writing, I offer thanks and bid a fond farewell. And now—THEY WENT THATAWAY!!!!

Acknowledgments

To Robert Cotton for his contributions in shaping the George O'Brien and Reb Russell sections; to Anthony Phillips, Cyril Nicholls and Harold Kinkade Jr. for the use of illustrative material, and to Larry Edmunds Bookshop and the Academy of Motion Picture Arts and Sciences—thank you all.

Riders of the Range

Bob Allen

WHEN ONE STOPS TO REFLECT UPON THE LARGE NUMBER OF B WESTERN actors who come to mind in any discussion of the sagebrush epics of the thirties and forties, one also arrives at the rather fascinating conclusion that no other film genre endowed its heroes with fame quite so rapidly. It was entirely possible for a good actor to labor for several years in dramatic subjects without ever having felt the glitter of stardust on his shoulders, yet donning a Stetson, strapping on a pair of six-shooters and climbing into the saddle almost immediately did the trick. Even more interesting is the fact that the number or quality of horse operas in which he appeared seldom had anything to do with his reputation; he was a western "star" and to the multitude of devotees who savor memories of long-lost Saturday matinees, that was sufficient to earn him a place in the nostalgic history of the B western.

One such gentleman was Irving Theodore Baer, a Mount Vernon, New York, boy who enjoyed the good fortune of having attended Dartmouth concurrent with Richard Dix's filming of *The Quarterback;* like several others included within the pages of this volume, Baer appeared as an extra in the film. Two more colleges figured in his education before Baer looked around for an occupation, and in rather rapid succession he worked as a bank clerk, professional artist and pilot for a flying service. But in 1931, the wanderlust bug bit him and Baer headed for Hollywood, where he managed to obtain a screen test at Warners that landed him a contract and a screen career in a series of society dramas. Now known as Robert Allen, Baer's career at Warners languished on the vine and so he made a horizontal move

Bob Allen.

from screen to Los Angeles stage shows, a move that quickly returned him to New York in a number of Broadway plays like *Society Girl* and *Holiday*.

Still working as Robert Allen, he was rediscovered by Columbia in 1934 and offered another Hollywood contract. This time with a fling at the bright lights of theatre marquees. This and the promise of better roles than he had enjoyed earlier at Warners brought Allen back to the West Coast, where he resumed his sound stage dramatics in a variety of drawing room dramas and melodramatic crime pictures. While under contract to Columbia, Bob discovered the world of Tim McCoy, that seemingly ageless portrayer of western heroism, and a strange fascination set in—this appeared to be the most obvious road to screen stardom that one could find. After undertaking a few appearances in some of McCoy's westerns, a hasty conference with Harry Cohn followed and Bob stepped into the saddle in 1936, spending two seasons chasing the baddies around the Southern California landscape.

Bob's Columbia westerns began as well-mounted productions revolving around the activities of the fabled Texas Rangers (a built-in interest factor for the small fry) and occasionally featured Jack Perrin as his sidekick instead of some comic left-over from the defunct fun factories. Although he was not a singer by any stroke of the imagination, some tasteless soul at Columbia insisted upon including the apparently required musical numbers; worse yet, he had Allen warble a few ditties himself, a practice that was soon halted. When Bob first appeared on the set of *Unknown Ranger,* his initial starring assignment, director Spencer G. Bennet (a veteran of many years of coaching non-actors past the camera) almost fell over backward. Bob delivered his lines like a real actor, something practically unheard of for many B western stars of the thirties, and this proved a real treat for the talented action director.

But as times went on, Bob Allen became the victim of two factors: a somewhat colorless personality as an action-adventure star and inane script writing. *Rangers Step In* called for him to escape from two husky guards by knocking them out before making his getaway. On-screen, the escape was managed with what appeared to be a gentle shove by the hero before diving through a window, mounting his conveniently placed horse and hustling off without further interference from the law. *Ranger Courage* opened with a wagon train moving through Texas under the escort of the State Rangers. No attempt was made to explain why this escort was required, nor was the audience told the reason why the wagon train was carrying a large box filled with cash; but the money provided the motive for outlaws dressed up as Indians to attack the travelers, which in turn brought Bob into action. I guess you could say it served its purpose even though the logic lapses were great ones.

But loopholes like these loomed large with the popcorn trade, who expected at least a minimum of reason to accompany their western fare. True, the kids weren't the most discriminating audiences in the world, and it's also true that many producers catered to what they genuinely felt to be a 12-year-old mentality; but you can only go so far before even the 12-year-olds revolt, and this seems to have happened to Bob. Trade reviewers suggested that Allen might do well to hustle back to drawing room drama before his few remaining fans there realized where he had disappeared to and what he was doing. By comparing program westerns to program melodrama in this vein, you can realize some of the status problems that lesser known sagebrush stars lived under. Taking the hint, Bob moved back to drama with Fox at the close of the 1937 season, retiring to the stage two years later where he enjoyed a quite successful career during the forties; but strangely enough, his major fame in the entertainment world stems from the short two years he spent on horseback at Columbia.

Former silent star Jack Perrin appeared in many of Bob's westerns. This is from **Reckless Ranger** (1937).

Jack Ingram, Jay Wilsey and Jack Rockwell with Bob in **Rangers Step In** (1937).

Reckless Ranger (1937).

The title changed (**Rio Grande Ranger**) but the casts remained the same.

Allen's experience on the stage and in B melodramas of the period made him a better dramatic performer than most western stars of the thirties.

Rex Allen

ONE OF THE LAST AND MOST SUCCESSFUL STARS TO ENTER THE PROGRAM western after World War II, Rex Allen's screen career proved to be a short-lived affair, yet he was popular enough to hold the distinction of being the last of the sagebrush stars to have left the Republic lot. An Arizona boy who had won a talent contest that set him on the musical road, Rex had moved East after finishing his education, and by 1940 he was a featured country and western singer on WTTM, a New Jersey radio station. His musical career eventually found him headlining the National Barn Dance after the war and he was just beginning to find popularity as a recording artist when along came Republic Pictures with an offer to immortalize him on the screen.

Returning West, Rex began his motion picture career with the starring role in *Arizona Cowboy* in 1949. Allen's oaters were well-mounted productions which closely rivaled those of Roy Rogers, the reigning cowpoke on Republic's range at the time. In fact, several of his early films came from scripts which had been written with Roy in mind and it was clear that Republic realized the potential box-office attraction of the slender, ruggedly handsome singer. Allen had several things working for him that offset his shortcomings as an actor; an excellent voice, a personable appeal and an infectious charm that easily won audiences to his side. The day of the musical western as it had been created in the thirties was now over and the Rex Allen westerns contained a balance of action, melodrama and music that seemed to suit the tastes of postwar horse opera fans.

Rex's Republic westerns were often in color, an added box-office

21

Rex Allen.

attraction in a day when other producers gleefully advertised their productions in "glowing sepiatone." (Such attempts to avoid the commonplace of black and white while also avoiding the additional cost of color, failed to make much of an impression on audiences). But good supporting casts included Slim Pickens as his sidekick, and attractive leading ladies were provided for the rather brief romantic interludes (most of which revolved around a musical number) that were also characteristic of Rex's westerns. Last but hardly least, Allen's scripts contained story value above and beyond the usual variation on a theme found in most of his competition's pictures. In one word, the Rex Allen westerns had quality, that unusual factor which occasionally appeared when the studio realized that it had a star whose popularity could be successfully exploited to enhance the earnings of his films.

Overshadowing Rocky Lane, Monte Hale and others, Rex quickly became the #2 cowboy on the Republic lot, and while Roy Rogers had little to fear from the newcomer, Rex gave the studio executives a comfortable feeling, as they knew that if Rogers were to walk out on them at any time, there was someone who could easily take his place as "The King of the Cowboys." To a large degree, this security factor was responsible for the continuation of quality in Rex's pictures; where other sagebrush stars had started off in well-done features, many had faded when the studio for some reason lost interest and the quality slid downhill. In a Hollywood known more for the magnitude of its blunders than its common sense, the fact that Republic recognized Allen's value is somewhat unusual. But it should be pointed out here that those responsible for the program pictures were by far a different breed than the self-proclaimed artists working on the larger budget films up the street. Their product was the bread-and-butter and made the money that allowed the expensively mounted and artistic endeavors to be produced. Of course, Republic made few such extravaganzas, but the men drawn to its studio were competent craftsmen (not artists) who took pride in working with a winning team, and with Rex Allen and Slim Pickens they had just such a combination.

But increasing costs, shrinking markets and television were taking their toll of program oaters and despite the use of reissues with new films as a means of filling out a season's series, stock footage used in place of shooting new sequences, and other economies to reduce costs, the end of the road was in sight for the B western. In the face of all this, it was even more unusual that the Allen series maintained quality as long as it did. Rex became the final contract cowboy at Republic, and when his series was discontinued he returned to radio and recording work, mixing in personal appearance tours before turning up on *Frontier Doctor,* a television series of the mid-fifties. Unlike others who had come to the screen with little or no acting experience, Rex had learned to cope with the camera, and while he became rather proficient at his art near the end, music remained his first love. More fortunate than Sunset Carson and some of the other Republic cowboys, he had a career to which he could and did turn.

Rex made his screen debut in **The Arizona Cowboy** with gorgeous Teala Loring in support. Republic then billed him as "The Arizona Cowboy" in subsequent westerns.

Slim Pickens rode as Rex's sidekick and provided the comic relief.

Every "Rider of the Range" had his own horse with which he was identified. This is Koko, Miracle Horse of the Movies, in action.

In stories like **Rodeo King and the Senorita** (1951), Rex mixed traditional western settings with modern western living, meeting with almost as much success with the formula as had Roy Rogers.

June Vincent, specialist in nasty villainess roles, appeared in many of Rex's westerns. Her cold beauty and icy reserve made her much in demand in program westerns like **Colorado Sundown** (1951).

The Last Musketeer (1952) with Mary Ellen Kay and Art Bridge.

Scenes like this from Republic's **Old Overland Trail** (1953) were artificial and contributed heavily to criticism of the musical western.

. . . but Rex balanced his music with action galore, fighting villains on one hand . . .

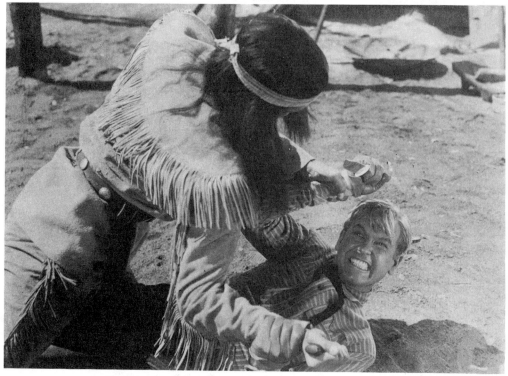

. . . and Indians on the other, all within the five short reels.

Allen staged some dandy fight scenes, like this one from **Thunder in God's Country** (1951) . . .

. . . or this from **Colorado Sundown** (1951).

Who wouldn't defend beautiful Jeanne Cooper under the **Shadows of Tombstone** (1953)?

Gene Autry

ALTHOUGH ROY ROGERS LAID CLAIM TO THE TITLE "KING OF THE COW-
boys," it more appropriately describes the life and times of Gene
Autry, a native Texan who called Oklahoma home. Of the singing
cowboys who rode on to the screen before World War II, few held
a candle to Autry's popularity and certainly none approached his business acumen. While it's true that Gene left much to be desired as an
actor, was only a marginal action-adventure performer and but a fair
musician, he managed to combine these qualities in a unique package
that spelled cash and plenty of it wherever he appeared.

Leaving behind him a growing career as a radio performer and
recording artist for the National Barn Dance, Gene came to the screen
in 1934 with Smiley Burnette (a hefty rural comic and singer) with
small roles in a Ken Maynard serial, *Mystery Mountain,* followed by
guest appearances in Maynard's feature, *In Old Santa Fe.* Gene and
his sidekick were then cast in *The Phantom Empire,* a Mascot serial
combining a western background with the science-fiction popular in
serial thrillers at the time. Gene played a radio star who broadcast
his show live from the ranch, which just happened to conceal an
unknown underground kingdom. Shady promoters were mixed up in
the suspense and each episode found Autry narrowly escaping from
the villains' clutches to make his broadcast on time. Produced by Nat
Levine's Mascot Pictures, whose rapid pacing and frantic action made
its serials among the best of the thirties, *The Phantom Empire* was
quite popular and evolved an entirely new approach to the western,
launching Autry on a long and fantastically successful career as a
screen cowboy.

31

Despite severe handicaps as an actor and adventure star, Gene Autry became the most successful cowboy of the talkie era and in popularity at least, successor to the fading Tom Mix's title as "America's Champion Cowboy." With Ann Rutherford and friend in a scene from **Melody Trail** (1935).

With the sole exception of *Shooting High,* which he made for Fox, Gene always played himself. His pictures managed to blend the old and new West together in a rather nervous combination—it was not at all unlikely to find a posse on horseback chasing outlaws escaping in an automobile. Quite adept at song writing,[1] Autry fashioned a musical format within the western framework, and to kids in the matinee audiences nothing seemed strange about watching Gene and his horse Champion returning at a leisurely pace after saving the heroine from a runaway wagon, singing his heart out to the accompaniment of the Cass County Boys, who were nowhere to be seen. The entire effect was slightly ludicrous, yet Autry achieved a tremendous popularity in a very short time. Under contract to Columbia Recording, a subsidiary of Republic Pictures (which had absorbed Mascot), Gene became the first western screen star to use radio's full potential as a means of furthering his movie career and drew as many adults to his pictures as small fry.

By 1936, the musical content of his pictures had been expanded until it almost overwhelmed the traditional western action. Reviewers complained that of the 58-minute running time of *Guns and Saddles,* the first 30 minutes were spent establishing the locale and letting Autry unlimber his vocal cords, leaving slightly less than one-half of the picture for the plot to take place. While Gene's early westerns were made for as little as $15,000, his budgets were soon increased and the extra money was used to flesh out the musical ingredients. His screen character was not really complex; Gene represented the good guy who tried to settle disputes peacefully, but once such means were exhausted, he relied upon fists and guns to do the job. A square-shooter all the way, Autry took a fair amount of punishment before resorting to violence, but when he faced the villains on their own ground, no amount of deception or foul play could prevent Gene from meting out justice. It was all a bit unreal, like the superheroes of the comic books, but the predictability of such a character was comforting, and with the comic relief of Smiley Burnette (and later Pat Buttram) to break up the monotony of the non-action sequences, the entire mishmash took on a form and shape imitated by countless others, few of whom enjoyed any large measure of success.

But there were other elements to these films which set them apart from the competition. They were made by Republic, which had inherited the fast-action philosophy from Mascot, and a crew of capable stuntmen provided the required action. Ernie Miller at the camera captured the scenic locales in a breathtaking manner not usually found in B westerns and William Lava and Cy Feuer contributed strong

---

1. Gene wrote an estimated 275 songs, the most popular of which were "You're The Only Star in My Blue Heaven" and "Be Honest With Me." He collaborated on another hit, "Silver Haired Daddy."

original musical scores. These factors all combined to ease the burden of Gene's writers, who found it difficult if not impossible to keep the star busy. Betty Burbridge voiced it this way, "How could you *write* for Gene? He was a very nice chap who never complained but there was little he could *do,* so you wrote a subplot for the rest of the cast to provide the action and inserted the star occasionally to sing a song. Sound simple? Try it sometime."

Offering a new path for the western at a time when the screen was overcrowded with sagebrush tales, Gene's overwhelming acceptance breathed new life into a genre that some have called America's only art form, and in 1939 he was one of the top 10 box-office attractions of the year. It was a sad day for his fans when Gene unbuckled the six-guns, trading Champion for an Air Corps transport while he served as a pilot in the China-Burma-India Theatre during World War II. Gene had shrewdly viewed himself not as a movie star or recording artist alone but as a genuine show business personality; and his personal appearances at fairs and rodeos provided the cement which held his career together, allowing him to amass a personal fortune at the same time. Although quite colorless as a western actor, Gene's personality came alive at personal appearances and those who attended his performances on the county fair circuits invariably came away devoted fans (especially the females), much to the surprise of his writers, knowledgeable artisans (some would prefer the term hacks) of the craft who continued to wonder how much longer the façade could be maintained. But removed from the reality of the situation, as were many of his detractors, they were unable to comprehend the special magic that Gene Autry could work on a live audience with his guitar and a few songs.

As Autry was actually merchandising himself to the public, he found it quite easy to step back in the saddle after discharge from military service, resuming a career which had remained in suspended animation while those of his competitors had been shattered by their absence from the screen during the war years. Nor did the advent of new faces hinder his career; Gene was able to leave Republic and the screen in protest over the studio's boosting of Roy Rogers and return even stronger. By 1949, he was making six pictures a year, spending seven months on public appearances and doing a weekly radio show in addition.

When Gene became his own producer in the late forties and moved his releases to Columbia, the heavy emphasis on the musical element was abandoned as too costly and a semblance of reality returned to the Autry westerns. Cinecolor was used in *The Strawberry Roan* and *The Big Sombrero,* but economics forced a cut-back on both fronts—scripts became shorter and the color turned into a sepia tone appropriately billed as Monocolor. Autry found a new interest and one that forever ended speculation as to whether he was an actor masquerading as a businessman or vice-versa. Television proved an entirely new market for his product and the venerable westerns were a sure-fire bet. Forming Flying A Productions while still producing for theatrical release, Gene masterminded five popular tv series, including one in which he and Pat Buttram starred. When exhibitors howled that Gene Autry on tv at no charge would destroy their paying clientele for his theatrical westerns, Gene countered with the shrewd argument that his tv segments would create new business for theatres; but he also recognized that the days of the inexpensive western were drawing to a close and that television alone would provide the only profitable outlet for such. These were good years for the Autry empire; he cut two discs, "Frosty the Snowman," and "Rudolph the Red-Nosed Reindeer," which outsold his long string of hit records by several million.

In a career spanning two decades, Gene Autry became both a household name and a millionaire, investing in hotels, radio and tv stations, music publishing, real estate and the California Angels baseball team among other ventures. Almost completely retired from public life now, he broke a self-imposed exile in 1970 to appear on several tv talk shows, but unlike other show business veterans past their prime, he had the good taste to resist the hosts' urgings that he sing, preferring to watch clips from his early films and simply reminisce.

Even at this late date, Gene still has a few detractors left, but none can deny that the commodity he packaged and merchandised was clean, wholesome entertainment. While his screen hero didn't frequent saloons and shied away from hard liquor, that didn't make him a sissy or weakling, but like the character created by Tom Mix, pointed out another way to live. Gene was good and his opponents were evil, and to kids who were unable to handle the fine shadings between these two, the moral lesson was clear. While it might seem peculiar to the generation of today, most of us welcomed and accepted the Autry philosophy that it wasn't a bad world after all and could be made better if every man stood up for his beliefs, even if we didn't care for the singing.

Republic bought top songs like **Tumbling Tumbleweed** (1935) for Gene, whose early pictures seldom found him without the ever-present guitar.

Smiley Burnette came to the screen as Gene's sidekick and while he supported other horse opera heroes in his lengthy career, is still remembered best as "Frog" Millhouse. With Gene and Dorothy Dix in **Guns and Guitars** (1936).

No wonder J. P. McGowan and Tom London are surprised; Gene's got a six-shooter instead of a guitar in **Guns and Guitars** (1936).

Radio and personal appearances helped to create an audience for westerns like **Gaucho Serenade** (1940) with Duncan Renaldo and went a long way in founding the Autry legend.

The early Autry westerns featured scenic locations and imaginative photography. **Blue Montana Skies** (1939) was typical.

Autry westerns like **Colorado Sunset** (1939) were devoted almost entirely to music, with plot playing a secondary role. The majorettes were Gwen Stith, Betty Atkinson and Maxine Conrad.

Gene demonstrates his western skills for a youthful Jane Withers in **Shooting High,** a 1940 Fox production.

In **Shooting High,** Gene played Wild Bill Carson, cowboy hero, instead of himself but despite the name, it was the same Autry. Jane Withers, Tom London and a young Jack Carson can be easily spotted.

Gene and Lynne Roberts in **Saddle Pals** (1947).

Twilight on the Rio Grande (1947), with Martin Garralaga.

Postwar Autry westerns like **Indian Territory** (1950) were not quite the musical comedies of earlier years, especially once Gene left Republic to produce his own for Columbia release.

Bob Cason takes it on the chin as Gregg Barton looks on in **Wagon Train** (1952).

Hills of Utah (1951).

Bob Baker

FOR SEVERAL DECADES, YOUNGSTERS ACROSS THE NATION (ESPECIALLY THE girls) vicariously enjoyed daydreams about fame and fortune befalling them in a peculiar manner—as they sipped their sodas, a rather innocuous looking fellow dressed in a business suit sauntered by and whispered "You ought to be in pictures," setting the glorious merrygoround of Hollywood stardom in motion. While it happened that way rarely (just enough times to fire their imagination and prove that it could), the American public entered all sorts of contests and mailed thousands of pictures to movie producers, hoping that the big break would come their way, and for a few it did.

Leland Weed owed his brief screen career to just such a quirk of fate. An Iowa boy who grew up in Arizona and Colorado, Leland punched cattle on a Colorado ranch for awhile after finishing school and it was here that one of the local wits nicknamed him "Tumble." Numerous odd jobs followed, leading him to the rodeo world, where he became quite adept at performing the variety of arts involved in this big-time application of show business to the West. Along the way, he coaxed music out of cooperative vocal cords and eventually arrived at the jumping-off point for most of the major country and western talent in the thirties, the National Barn Dance.

By 1936, the musical cowboy rage was on in earnest and the screen had been deluged with songbirds of the West, but Universal announced that it was in the market for still another. Leland's mother sent in a picture of her son with a brief letter noting his accomplishments and to everyone's great surprise (except Mrs. Weed's), a letter

43

Glenn Strange, Jimmie Philips and Jack Kirk menace Bob Baker in **The Last Stand** (1938).

came back inviting him to make a screen test. Leland headed for Hollywood, and once the test was viewed Universal didn't take long in deciding to put him under contract—here was a tall, rugged looking individual who not only met all the usual requirements for western heroics, but in addition could really ride, rope and sing as well. A bit shaky at this turn of events, Weed signed the contract and then looked up an old acquaintance from rodeo days, Max Terhune; Max had forsaken the rodeo scene for Hollywood and seemed to be doing well enough in supporting roles. Terhune coached the new leading man and Universal decided to rename him Bob Baker, which raises no end of speculation as to the creativity on the big U lot at that time.

Bob Baker hit the matinee screen in 1937 with *Courage of the West,* and while yet another song thrush in western costume didn't set too well with *Variety,* the trade paper commented favorably on his appearance while bemoaning the fact that any reasonable facsimile of a cowpoke who wanted to succeed on the screen was required to sing or face catastrophe at the box-office. As Baker came on the scene with good looks, a pleasing personality and a fair voice, it was expected that he'd go a long way in this new career, but put to the test with a potential new star on its lot, Universal flubbed in film after film until even music was unable to save the Baker series from oblivion.

Unfortunately for Bob, the celluloid range was swamped with musical talent by 1938 and the ability to croon under the stars by a campfire was no longer the governing factor in the success or failure of an individual actor. Plot line and production values were slowly regaining their rightful place as determining factors and only Gene Autry and Roy Rogers were able to disregard story for songs and get away with it. In addition to the general market conditions, Baker's western schedule was plagued with indecision on the part of his producers, who couldn't seem to agree exactly what image they really wanted to put forth with him. For a time, Bob rode with Fuzzy Knight at his side, but before long he acquired another sidekick in the form of a trained dog, causing reviewers and fans to shudder at the prospects of another new trend (two dumb animals are better than one cowboy) sweeping the sagebrush screen; Jack Luden at Columbia had started it when he added a dog as a regular performer and here was Baker apparently following suit. But their fears were unfounded and the silent era's cycle of cowboy, horse and dog trios did not materialize, nor did Baker's series last much longer.

One would not think that a major studio like Universal would have so badly botched the new star's build-up, but they did and before long, Bob surfaced in the Johnny Mack Brown westerns at the same studio. He and Brown were supposed to be "The Frontier Marshals" but Bob's major effort came in the musical department. In 1941, he left Universal to join Monogram in its "Trail Blazers" series, which featured old-timers Hoot Gibson and Ken Maynard as the leads, but once again he was frustrated by shoddy production values and well-traveled plots. When his contract expired in 1943, he simply left the screen.

As the program western was carefully devised to return a maximum on a minimum investment, there was little incentive to invest more time and money than necessary to produce a marketable product—the competition was so keen at that time that the proper attention to turn out a better product often went unrewarded. This type of screen fare would earn a certain rental and no more—higher production costs meant either higher rental rates or a smaller net profit, and either way the extra money invariably involved meant diminishing returns. Few western stars commanded the audience attention to overcome "the system" and so Bob Baker became another of its victims.

Bob rode with Fuzzy Knight in many of his Universal westerns.

Guilty Trail (1938).

Bob with Forrest Taylor in **Prairie Justice.**

Every Baker western had a song fest like these from **The Last Stand** . . .

. . . and **Vigilante War.** That's pretty Frances Robinson listening to Bob.

But LeRoy Mason doesn't even care to discuss the matter. Suppose he hated singing cowboys? From **Outlaw Express.**

Donald Barry

ONE OF THE UNWRITTEN REQUIREMENTS FOR WESTERN STARDOM HELD
that the hero must be tall, slender and fair. In addition, he was required
to ride a horse, draw a gun faster than his opponent, occasionally
thrash the daylights out of a villain or two, and depending upon the
producer for whom he worked, a fairly decent singing voice might
also be in order. All of these could be faked to one degree or another,
but his size and build was most important to the heroic image, for the
star was the product of good clean living whose emotional makeup
allowed him only decent thoughts—and this had to project from the
screen. But despite this rule of thumb, two western actors rose to
prominence: Bob Steele[1] and Donald Barry.

An orphan born in Houston, Texas, Barry was a little short on both
stature (he stood 5', 8½") and looks, but like Steele he won an immense
following in the early forties. Don still tells the story of how he broke
into pictures after attending the Texas School of Mines. Walking onto
the RKO lot, he took charge of a chorus line, acting as an assistant
producer until his deception was discovered. With this introduction
to the world of make-believe, Barry decided that acting might not be
a bad way of earning a living. Landing a spot in a touring company
performing *Tobacco Road*, he picked up the fundamentals of acting
and soon appeared back at RKO, making his screen debut with a bit
role in *Night Waitress* (1936). From there, it was a short journey to
Republic and western roles beginning with *Wyoming Outlaw*.

---

1. Steele's career was discussed at length in my *Winners of the West*, A. S. Barnes
& Co., 1970.

Don "Red" Barry in **The Sombrero Kid.**

Don hit the big time in 1940 when Republic decided to star him as *Red Ryder* in a series of oaters based upon the exploits of Fred Harmon's popular comic strip hero. Why Donald Barry, no one seems to remember, but it was a most unusual bit of casting. The fictional Ryder was tall and slender, as all good heroes are supposed to be; Don was short and inclined to be a bit on the heavy side when not watching his weight. In no way did he even remotely resemble the favorite of millions of comic strip fans, yet Barry and little Tommy Cook, who played the Indian boy Little Beaver, hit it off with matinee audiences from the very beginning.

Don's husky voice set him apart from other western stars, as did his stature; but what he lacked in size was more than compensated for by his intestinal fortitude. Like Bob Steele, Don "Red" Barry was one of the best scrappers to appear in the B westerns. A hair-trigger temper could be touched off by any little thing and the drop of a fighting word turned Barry into a virtual miniature hurricane, with fists flying in every direction. Don put everything he had into the role —while other stars mounted their horses with grace, or if the occasion warranted it jumped onto the saddle, Don Barry literally flung himself into position with a vengeance unmatched by any other sagebrusher. His draw was fast and slapping leather against Don could only lead to grief, a comfortable feeling for those of us rooting in the front seats.

If there was such a thing as a "method" school of acting in those days, Don Barry could be considered a leading exponent; you really believed that he was living the role. Not exactly handsome, but good-looking in a sense of the word, Don had the appearance of an outlaw written all over his face. When the situation became tense and Don clenched his lips together tightly, he looked for all the world like a shifty scoundrel whose determination would see him through any rough spots. The realism of casting Barry as the underdog on whom all suspicion fell was heightened by this appearance—while Charles Starrett, Johnny Mack Brown and others were far too virtuous looking to be real badmen, or even successfully pretend to be, such a script proved to be Barry's forte. He performed equally well as hero or villain and was one of the few B western stars who came across convincingly while masquerading as an outlaw. I suspect that this departure from the usual blandness associated with western heroism was a good part of Barry's appeal for those of us in the matinee audience who had come to regard the hero as one who conquered injustice because he was a bit smarter than the villains and needed only to wait for the scriptwriter to straighten everything out to satisfaction as the final reel was flashed on the screen. It always seemed as if Barry was one step ahead of his writers although he really wasn't; they just had a more colorful personality to work with. The combination of these elements—size, looks, personality and enthusiasm—made Don "Red" Barry stand out for a time far above his competitors, placing him in the ranks of the western heroes whose pictures were most appreciated on warm Saturday afternoons.

During World War II, Don took time out from acting to entertain the troops, with Bill Elliott replacing him as Red Ryder. Barry tried his hand at straight drama during the war years with appearances in *The Purple Heart* and several other good pictures; in 1945 he returned to the screen in a series of dramas and westerns for Lippert, which did little to put his career back in gear. After starring in a few rough and ready roles, he had returned to the saddle, but it was almost over. The Lippert westerns were poorly scripted and badly produced, when compared to Don's earlier Republic pictures; the youthful Barry of a few years before had been bushwhacked and the fans had not remained around to rescue him.

He formed Donald Barry Productions to produce for television in 1951 but this venture failed to work out as planned and his starring career virtually ended with an independent oater called *Jesse James'*

Women. Produced, directed and starring Don, this picture was partially financed by the citizens of Prentiss, Missouri, and was filmed by a Chicago technical crew. Released through United Artists in 1954, reviewers had a field day with the story line (a bit more frankness and it would have made a whale of an X-rated film today) which found Jesse James (Don) irresistible to one female after another. The sets were skimpy, even by B western standards, and it showed the results of corner-cutting; the most action and best fights were among the lady performers.

Dropping the nickname, Donald Barry became an oft-seen character actor on television, appearing in many shows as a private detective, police officer and sometimes even on the other side of the law. Recently, he came back into the news with an unusual proposition to his former fans. TV stations around the nation still run his feature westerns and rank him second only to John Wayne in popularity as reflected by viewers' letters. On the strength of this and in the face of an entertainment industry desperately crying for pure entertainment instead of sex on the screen (but doing nothing to alter the course of events), Don has come to believe that a return to the heroics he once performed is in the wings. Wire services carried his proposal around the nation and money began to arrive in the mail. Don believes that if each of his fans donated $1.00 to the cause (making them shareholders), he could raise $1½ million to produce six westerns for theatrical and tv release. At this writing, the money is still coming in and being deposited in trust in a bank; whether his plans will work out or not remains to be seen, but while he is not alone among the former western greats who think a return to the screen heroics of the forties is desirable, he is the only one doing anything to bring it about. Who knows? Don "Red" Barry may well overcome the financial obstacle as he overcame so many others on the screen, but in spite of his determination it all rests in the hands of his fans this time instead of a scriptwriter's story treatment.

Don's early westerns were among his best. A rough, tough scrapper, he vowed to Sid Saylor and sheriff Ed Cassidy that he'd find the man responsible in **Wyoming Wildcats** (1941).

Barry's roles often called for him to play the bad guy, a portrayal in which he was highly effective.

Action was a keynote of Don's westerns.

Which way did they go in **Wyoming Wildcat**? Don'll find out!

Ed Cobb met his match in little Don Barry.

Peggie Castle and Don in **Jesse James' Women** (1954).

William Boyd

ONLY ONE OF THE B WESTERN STARS EVER BECAME SO CLOSELY IDENTIFIED with his screen character that his personal identity was almost totally submerged in the alter ego. Born William Boyd in Cambridge, Ohio in 1898, he was known far and wide to the popcorn trade of the thirties and forties as Hopalong Cassidy, although Boyd's screen career had actually started in 1919, when he appeared as an extra in Cecil B. deMille's *Why Change Your Wife?* By the close of the twenties, he was an established star of the silent screen, playing romantic leads in deMille adventure epics. Bill Boyd had one other qualification which he shared only with Randolph Scott and a select few of the other program western heroes—he could really act and the series that brought him lasting fame and a good-sized fortune allowed him to do just that.

Producer Harry Sherman, who had obtained the rights to film Clarence E. Mulford's stories of the West, early in 1935 suggested to Boyd that he might like to play the role of Buck Peters in the initial film. Boyd, whose star had dimmed somewhat in the early talkies (romantic leads were a dime a dozen), read the script and agreed to appear in the picture, but only if he could play the character of Hopalong. As originally conceived, Cassidy was a game-legged, hard-drinking roustabout foreman, a characterization that could not be truthfully translated to the screen in those pre-Lee Marvin–George Kennedy days; and certainly it was not a heroic one. However Boyd talked Sherman into giving him the role, and in the summer of 1935 the first of 54 westerns produced by Sherman, released by Paramount

William Boyd in **The Eagle's Brood** (1935), second of the Hopalong
Cassidy westerns for Harry Sherman. The lady leaning on the bar was
Joan Woodbury, who also worked under the name Nana Martinez.

(and later United Artists) and starring Bill Boyd as Cassidy made
its debut.

In portraying Hopalong Cassidy, Boyd retained the game leg
during the initial film (it was explained in the second as the result of
a bullet wound which had healed) and although greeted by reviewers
with mixed emotions, one of the western screen's legendary characters was off and running. Much of the physical action was given
to Jimmy Ellison, who created the role of Hoppy's sidekick Johnny
Nelson in the first eight films, but while he was to star in his own
series of oaters years later for Monogram, Ellison was considered
as one of the weak points in the early films. He was retained mainly
to relieve Hoppy of the action sequences and romantic interest. In
1937 Russell Hayden replaced him and "Johnny Nelson" became

"Lucky Jenkins." George "Gabby" Hayes had joined the cast in 1936 to portray "Windy Halliday," and until the close of the 1940 season, Hoppy rode with Hayden and Hayes at his side.

A quite distinguished figure usually dressed in black and riding a snow white horse, Boyd projected as soft-spoken and retiring, presenting more the father figure than the hard-riding, rough-fighting stereotype western hero; on some occasions he even came across as a genuine gentleman. His white hair (which he had acquired by the time he was 21) lent an extra dignity to his portrayal, giving Hoppy the authority of age lacked by so many among the competition. Unlike the somewhat garish costuming affected by other western stars, the plain garb lent a no-nonsense posture to the Cassidy image. We never worried about Hoppy taking time out to warble a tune or romance the leading lady; Boyd played the role straight and left the musical comedy interludes (which were kept to a minimum anyway) to others. Altogether, it was a curious blend which gave the exciting and romantic chores to the sidekick and the rest to Boyd, yet left him as the hero in everyone's eyes.

The production values in these early Cassidy westerns were far above those of other B westerns, especially in terms of locations and photography, and the Hopalong Cassidy series became a welcome addition to the celluloid lore of the West. While we didn't realize it at the time, Boyd was a so-so rider and his early work made use of double Cliff Lyons in the chase and riding sequences which were filmed mainly with long shots, but by 1936 the star's skill on horseback had improved considerably, a fact evidenced by the inclusion of close-ups of him in the riding scenes. The action in the Cassidy westerns was quite limited except for gun fights, and sidekicks bore the burden of bruised knuckles.

Mulford's literary works were adhered to fairly closely in the early adaptations, giving them a story line above the ordinary, and Sherman's long experience in production was put to good use; the Hopalong Cassidy westerns began slowly and gradually accelerated as the reels rolled by, building up to a grandiose finish in the last reel. This slow, deliberate pacing was also exceptional, carrying audience interest with it and the camera work and good editing added to the overall excitement. But despite all these favorable attributes, the series was essentially a formula one, well produced and slickly packaged; but with a total of 66 features starring the same hero, it couldn't escape being otherwise.

Boyd kept his character completely in tune with the younger

audiences and nothing offensive ever appeared in a Cassidy western. While parents might frown upon the screen activities of some sagebrush heroes, Boyd shortly earned their complete respect and admiration, and no one in the neighborhood ever raised a defensive eyebrow when we announced that Hoppy was playing. This emphasis on wholesome screen fare earned Boyd a reputation that was to overwhelm his own personality; wherever he appeared in person, he was greeted as Hopalong.

While there was no attempt to portray the West in the realistic manner of Bill Hart, Cassidy's scripters did avoid going to the opposite extreme. In addition some of the series were almost 90 minutes in length, unusual for a B western. After Hayden took his leave in 1940, the sidekick was played by a number of young actors. At the same time, silent screen comic Andy Clyde replaced Hayes's "Windy Halliday" with a garrulous character called "California Carlson."

When Sherman terminated his association with the series in 1944, Hopalong Cassidy had presumably disappeared for good; but Boyd brought him back to the screen two years later, producing and starring in a dozen westerns during 1946–48. These low-budget affairs were among the saddest of the entire group from a story and action standpoint. Laughing when Boyd negotiated the rights to the entire lot of his old films, Hollywood pundits nearly choked when they realized that the star was more visionary than they had been. Mulford's publishers had retained the television rights in 1935 (a not uncommon clause despite the belief that TV is a postwar development—in fact several silent producers did the same thing in 1928–29) and Boyd correctly foresaw, as did Gene Autry, that the small box would soon be begging for programming.

The appearance of Hopalong Cassidy on television ignited an entire new wave of interest in the character and was marked by the advent of a tremendous avalanche of merchandising—comic books, toy guns, Hopalong Cassidy outfits, etc. Personal appearances at rodeos and circuses were tied into the boom, as was a reprinting of the Mulford novels, some of which were rewritten to reconcile the literary character to his accepted screen image. In the process, Bill Boyd went from a near-bankrupt producer to a millionaire—a fantastic but brief success story which ended with the star's well-deserved retirement after the conclusion of a 30-minute series made especially for television.

Jimmy Ellison carried the action and romance for Hoppy during the first season. This is from **Three on a Trail** (1936) with Muriel Evans.

Boyd and Ellison in **Call of the Prairie** (1936).

Brett Wood and Hoppy in **Stagecoach War** (1940).

Brett Wood, Hoppy and Russell Hayden in **Hidden Gold** (1940).

A youthful Robert Mitchum played villain in several of the Cassidy westerns. In **False Colors** (1940), he got his just reward as Andy Clyde looked on.

It's Mitchum again in **Hoppy Serves a Writ** (1943) . . .

. . . and again in **Riders of the Deadline** (1943).

Fool's Gold (1946) was the second release in the new Cassidy westerns produced by Boyd. Reviewers panned these low-budget oaters, claiming that Hoppy's character had changed. The lovely lady is Jane Randolph.

Johnny Mack Brown

ONE OF A GROUP OF ATHLETIC HEROES WHO STORMED THE FILM CAPITAL in the late twenties, Johnny Mack Brown carved out a substantial career, winning a place in football's Hall of Fame and a legion of devoted screen fans in a career which came to a close in 1966. A native of Dothan, Alabama, Johnny came West as a participant in the 1927 Rose Bowl and while in Pasadena he renewed a friendship with actor George Fawcett; the two had met in Birmingham the year before while Johnny was working as an extra in a film being shot there on location. When, through Fawcett, Brown met Erich Von Stroheim, the director commented that Johnny could easily become an actor if he wanted to and the football star returned to Hollywood in 1929 for a screen test and an M-G-M contract.

While Brown toyed occasionally with western roles, much of his early work included dramatic roles opposite Garbo, Pickford, Crawford and other leading ladies of equal calibre. But picked to play the lead in *Billy the Kid* (1930), Johnny was personally coached for the role by William S. Hart and his sensitive portrayal won unanimous approval. This was followed by the role of Berk Jarvis in *The Great Meadow* (1931), an M-G-M epic of Kentucky frontier life during the Revolutionary War. This received both a hilariously sarcastic review in *Variety* one day and a sober one the next, but Brown did not seriously entertain thoughts of western stardom until 1935, when he made several independent westerns for A. W. Haeckle, who released through Republic as well as his own company, Supreme.

Johnny Mack Brown in **The Great Meadow** (1931). (Photo by Clarence Sinclair Bull)

These routine stories suffered from erratic (mostly poor) direction and had little more to commend them than their star, who stood out handsomely. A considerably better actor than most of his western peers, Johnny was a huge likeable bear with a rich Southern drawl and the athletic ability to do much of his own action work. The Haeckle westerns led Brown to Universal, where he remained for several years.

Tall, good looking and all he-man, Johnny Mack Brown quickly surfaced above Universal's assembly line as one of the B western's leading exponents of the clean, virtuous life. Always the good guy or an undercover agent from start to finish, there was little chance of casting this Southern gentleman as anything else. Johnny just exuded those wholesome qualities that make a family hero, which worked to his advantage by attracting not only the kids as fans, but many of their parents as well.

Nothing seemed too great for Johnny Mack Brown to overcome, and taking advantage of his size and strength, script writers invariably involved him in a brawl from which he emerged unscathed and victorious after vanquishing a half dozen or more of the villain's henchmen single-handed. Counting up his screen fights, the man-to-man fistic duel appears to be a rarity in the Brown westerns, and the high point for all of us in the darkened theatres on any given Saturday afternoon was that moment when good old John finally made up his mind to stop fooling around and cleaned up the saloon, the town and the territory once and for all.

Johnny was no slouch in the saddle either; he could ride with the best and a Brown chase was always a lengthy thrill, ending in a flurry of fists as law and order was restored once again to whatever community the villains had been unfortunate enough to select for their nefarious activities. John never strayed too far from the traditional West; automobiles, airplanes and other modern devices were seldom seen but one concession was made in the opt-repeated format, especially in his post-war westerns. While Johnny tended to the business at hand and didn't bore us with attempts to sing, there was often a musical group of some kind around to beat out a ditty or two for those who insisted that cowboys in the old West must have done something more than run down rustlers, break up range wars, save the settlers from Indians and outlaws, and all those other tiring chores that seemed to be their lot. Most of us knew that cowboys did do other things, but it wasn't singing and it couldn't be shown on the screen in those days.

Constructed mainly by such skilled writers as George Pyper and Ford Beebe and directed by Ray Taylor and Lambert Hillyer, Johnny's Universal westerns were in good hands. While these men behind the scenes never received awards, they were experienced production veterans whose work had found favor with audiences for years. As such, they knew how to flesh out a routine story with action, adventure and sufficient style to place the finished product far above what the plot material deserved. Despite the fact that there are only a limited number of story variations available to work with, Johnny's series turned out consistently good, with fine musical scores and photography superior in its cinematic sense to that of other program westerns. While they were produced in the assembly-line manner at which Universal had become most proficient, the majority of his Universal oaters avoided this mass-production look, and stood up well at the box office. Toward the close of his stay at Universal, Johnny also co-starred with Tex Ritter and Bob Baker in some interesting adventures.

In 1942, he rose into the ranks of the 10 top western stars at the box office, where he remained until 1950. It was a Monogram series that brought and maintained this popularity. Monogram acquired Johnny for a series closely patterned after Buck Jones's style, and gave him Raymond Hatton in place of Fuzzy Knight as the ever-present sidekick required as part of the western formula picture. Hatton, a character actor rather than a comedian, made an excellent foil for Brown and the two developed an on-screen rapport that was reassuring to the small fry in the audience. After all, the sidekick was there to help the hero out in times of trouble, and he usually proved to be the sole link between life and death when the villains managed to bushwhack or capture the star.

In spite of the second-rate comic relief assigned this character in the scripts, he was important to the writers as a life-saving device which allowed them to really place the star's life in danger and then extract him logically albeit coincidentally with the sidekick's help. Those unfortunate enough to ride with lovable but incompetent Fuzzy Knight put their lives in extreme jeopardy; you never could tell what kind of trouble Fuzzy would get mixed up in all by himself, but Ray Hatton reversed the role and became an older, experienced right hand guiding the hero (instead of the hero planning his sidekick's every move) and projected a level-headed, shrewd image—one that could be depended upon completely in a stress situation. When Hatton rode for help, you could slump back in the seat and breathe a sigh of relief, knowing that he'd not only make it, but in near-record time. Unrealistic perhaps, but comforting all the same. Hatton rode with Johnny for several seasons before being gradually replaced by Max Terhune. Terhune might have been a tougher looking wrangler to face, but he was a throwback to the

"I'm in trouble again, Johnny" school and most of us preferred the independence of the grizzled Hatton.

The Johnny Mack Brown westerns reached their peak about this time, both in style and content. Johnny's popularity started to ebb as the forties faded and his age suddenly began to show noticeably. The star put on weight in the early fifties and with the lithe trim figure slipping away, many of his exploits seemed to lose their flavor. One of the few outstanding western stars of the sound era, Brown was caught between advancing age and the death of the theatrical western series, and informally hung up his gun belt in 1952.

Fans occasionally caught a glimpse of Johnny in minor roles despite a new career as host at one of Hollywood's night spots. But the new "adult" western format with its emphasis on psychology and violence found little use for overweight overaged good guys and Johnny Mack Brown finally crossed over to the side of lawlessness for a few roles before calling it a day in 1966 with a role in *Apache Uprising*. Though he was no longer even a shadow of the handsome slender athlete whose *Billy the Kid* had impressed Bill Hart, Brown rides on in the land of celluloid heroes as his western exploits are revived by collectors and the ever-growing band of western fans. That's the fascination of the cinema—the preservation of what once was, to be enjoyed over and over. If Johnny should occasionally wince when watching television today, it's probably a rerun of one of his starring films of so long ago, but he can take a measure of comfort in knowing that he's not alone—we all wince as the youthful Johnny Mack Brown carries us back to a carefree afternoon in our own lives.

Johnny and William S. Hart discuss a scene from **Billy the Kid** (1930). The gun in Hart's hand was a presentation to Brown and supposedly one of the Kid's original six-shooters.

A series for A. W. Hackett in 1935 put Johnny in the saddle for good.
From **The Courageous Avenger.**

With friend John Wayne in Paramount's **Born to the West** (1938).

Johnny had the drop on Harry Cording and Jack Rockwell as a terrorized Fuzzy Knight hoped for the best in **Bury Me Not on the Lone Prairie** (1940).

Johnny's football expertise came in handy in **Boss of Bullion City** (1940), as Dick Alexander bites the dust.

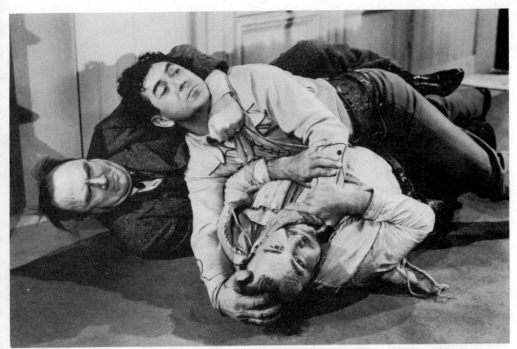

Harry Cording tangled with Brown often and Johnny's brawls were
always live affairs, as this one from **Rawhide Rangers** (1941).

Raiders of the South (1947).

Jennifer Holt, Johnny and Raymond Hatton in **Trigger Fingers** (1946).

Brown avoided gunplay when possible. He cautioned Max Terhune and Ray Hatton to holster the six-shooters in **Hidden Danger** (1948) . . .

. . . but when there was no other way, he took the challenge seriously. Myron Healey was usually on the receiving end. From **Outlaw Gold** (1950).

Colorado Ambush (1951).

Johnny's career was closed out in 1965 with roles in **The Bounty Killer** (above) and **Apache Guns.** Dan Duryea had the drop on sheriff Brown, but despite his age, Johnny's voice carried the same soft-spoken ring of authority.

Sunset Carson

THE STATE OF TEXAS SEEMED TO SEND MORE THAN ITS SHARE OF COWPOKES to the big city of Hollywood, where they soon appeared on movie screens around the nation, larger than life and complete with drawl, fighting every imaginable kind of skullduggery while winning the West all over again for the Lone Star State. Although their acting ability was often held up to question, all seemed to be strapping gentlemen of heroic proportions. However few made an impact as unnoticeable in celluloid life as one Michael Harrison, who walked onto the screen in 1943 when he was but a tender 22 and stayed until 1952, when the B western developed a noticeable case of the wheeze, and cowboys were cut loose from studio rosters to fend for themselves once more. A very few survived the upheaval by transferring their bunkhouses to television, more retired with some semblance of fame achieved during their careers, and a few fell into near-total obscurity. One of the latter was Mr. Harrison.

A strapping six-foot former rodeo champion with muscles to match, he first came to public attention as a G.I. in *Stagedoor Canteen*, but his was not the type of role calculated to make one an overnight sensation, nor was Harrison the kind of actor who could embue the part with qualities beyond those written in the script. Yet he turned up almost immediately at Republic, garbed in western finery and bearing a new name—Sunset Carson. Wearing a tall white Stetson and sitting astride his equally gigantic white mount, Sunset cut an imposing figure on the screen, one that was destroyed only when he got off the horse and read his lines.

77

Sunset Carson.

His earnest but hesitant delivery and the very broad drawl which accompanied it made it quite clear to anyone interested that this was indeed a real live Texan recently imported from the wide open spaces, and while Sunset mopped up the baddies with flailing fists, his pictures all had an unreality about them that made identification with their hero more difficult than with Charles Starrett or even Gene Autry. In one sense, they almost seemed to be giant put-ons despite the fact that each was as well-mounted as any Republic production of that era. Fast-moving action-packed tales of western derring-do, to be sure, but as one trade reviewer put it with tongue-in-cheek, Sunset played Sunset, which wasn't really a tough part at all. An intense stare which gave him the appearance of being slightly squint-eyed was coupled with a broad grin, providing his two basic histrionic poses; but armed with his six-shooters, fists and a bullwhip, Sunset fought his way around the West in colorfully titled epics like *Red River Renegades, The Cherokee Flash* and *Rio Grande Raiders*, his final Republic western.

The B western had started to feel the economic pinch of a declining market and increasing costs right after World War II ended and where a profusion of sagebrush stars had ridden the range during the thirties and early forties, their numbers declined rapidly as contracts expired in the latter part of the decade; Sunset was one of the first to become footloose and fancy free. He wound up with Astor Pictures in a series of badly written and poorly photographed horse operas, many of which were shot in 16mm to reduce costs. (Later they would be lab enlarged to 35mm for theatrical release.)

Sunset's career skidded to a halt in 1952, and when a projected television series failed to materialize (it seems that virtually everyone on the western screen had plans for the tube), he spent a couple of seasons with the Clyde Beatty Circus before fading over the horizon for the final time. It had been a good ride for the boyish looking Texan while it lasted, but unfortunately Carson really had little going for him other than a catchy name. Had his acting ability and screen personality developed as the films cranked by, he might have held on for another few years, but when it isn't there, it just isn't there; and there's not much you can do about it except retire gracefully, which Sunset did. Among B western fans who recall his era, Sunset Carson lives on in their memories, more for his colorful screen name than anything else.

The chap at the left in this scene from **Stage Door Canteen** (1943) was Michael Harrison, soon to be known to western fans as Sunset Carson.

Sunset always walked into trouble with his eyes open. Ed Cobb is about to close them in **Red River Renegades** (1946) . . .

But Sunset had his licks too, as Si Jenks tries to uncross his eyes.

Sunset frees Bob Wilke in **Bandits of the Badlands,** but it's all a ruse to get our boy in good with the baddies.

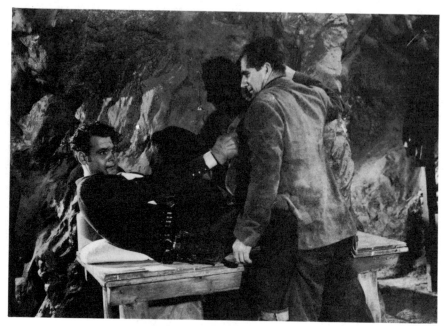

The El Paso Kid (1946).

If he has to, Sunset will thrash the answer from Fred Graham; Peggy Stewart almost seems pleased at the prospect. From **Bandits of the Badlands** (1945).

Frank Jaquet can trust Sunset, but can our hero trust him? **Santa Fe Saddlemates** (1945).

Roy Barcroft, Sunset, Linda Sterling and Olin Howlin in **Santa Fe Saddlemates** (1945).

Mary Carr, Peg Stewart, Sunset and Lee Shumway in **Oregon Trail** (1945).

Buster Crabbe

CLARENCE LINDEN CRABBE WAS AN UNLIKELY NAME FOR SCREEN STARDOM, yet as Buster Crabbe, this Olympic champion became a serial-western adventure hero whose exploits are still playing television and college film societies three decades later. A native of Oakland, California, Crabbe lived much of his early life in Hawaii, becoming a most proficient athlete whose second home was in the water. Educated at the University of Southern California, he won the 400-meter race in the 1932 Olympics and was signed shortly after as the star of *Tarzan the Fearless,* quite a change (at least in status) from his $12.50 a week job as a stock clerk. *King of the Jungle* followed for Paramount, and almost before he knew it, Buster was both a star of the inexpensive thrill epics and on his way to being typed as such.

After starring in a group of rather good westerns for Paramount, Buster was selected to play Flash Gordon in a 1936 Universal serial, a break that had a distinctive bearing on the direction of his career. While the acting required to play this popular comic strip hero on the screen wasn't great, the 23-year old Crabbe brought a zest and flavor to the role that greatly overshadowed his past popularity. Another Flash Gordon serial in 1938 and one as Buck Rogers in 1939 proved as immensely profitable to Universal, but practically brought his screen career to a roaring halt. Buster suddenly found himself restricted to roles he later described as "muscle man parts" and as the forties opened, about the only work he could find in Hollywood was as a heavy in low-budget melodrama or as a western hero. Trying a few of the former, he settled for a future in sagebrush drama and

85

Larry "Buster" Crabbe.

for several years, Buster Crabbe rode the range for Producers Releasing Corporation.

PRC westerns weren't noted for very much, but they did avoid the musical elements made popular by Autry and Rogers (except in the case of certain singing cowpokes like George Houston and Eddie Dean) and Buster's fans were spared suffering through breaks in the story's continuity while three or four yodelers warmed up (or cooled off) their vocal cords; the writers provided enough breaks of their own. Instead, audiences suffered through the nonsensical antics of Al "Fuzzy" St. John, who rode beside Buster through film after film.

PRC was St. John's home for years and the grizzled silent screen comic came as close to regaining stardom there as he had known in over a decade. As Buster's sidekick, Al provided a large element of comedy and many of the PRC westerns found him carrying the first reel or so all by himself, with the hero introduced later. Crabbe was cast as Billy the Kid in many, and while his scripters traded on the real Billy's reputation, there was really little resemblance to the original in the character Buster played. Some of the scripts proved to be almost low-comedy classics, with Buster playing both Billy and a look-alike badman, giving St. John fits trying to figure out who was whom, a problem sometimes shared by the audience.

As a western hero, Buster Crabbe deserved better. Gone was the boyish look of the Flash Gordon years, to be replaced by a ruggedly handsome profile more suitable to heroics. Still lean and trim, the youthful star kept his dialogue to a minimum (St. John made enough noise for both) and so projected as a rough, tough and taciturn westerner. Had Buster's scripts and the production work that translated them to the screen been better, he might have attracted an even larger following, but PRC represented the lower end of the sagebrush spectrum and the quality of his horse operas varied from good to bad, with the emphasis on the latter. Keeping costs low kept PRC in business and fancy trimmings like rehearsal, retakes, a variety of camera angles and script motivation were looked upon as luxuries not to be indulged in. If the scene didn't go quite right, you could always chalk it up to realism; after all, what real western hero could leap on his horse's back without missing once or twice during his career? Doubles were all over the place, and in many cases there was little or no attempt to hide the fact; yet Buster had his moments and made a rather believable hero despite the production shortcomings.

One of the few stars to recognize that television would have a profound impact on the B movies, Crabbe left motion pictures behind in 1948. Between 1946 and 50, he toured the United States and Europe with his own Aquaparade, and in 1950–51 appeared on New York's WOR-TV hosting an afternoon movie and doing his own morning physical culture show five days a week. Few were more qualified to help Bronx housewives work off the flab than the personable Buster Crabbe, who had acquired five world swimming records and 35 national championships by then. He produced and starred in his own television series, *Captain Gallant of the Foreign Legion,* for several years; operated a swimming pool company bearing his name; served as Aquatic Director for the Hotel Concord in New York's Catskills and more recently a licensed representative for a New York brokerage firm. But despite his success in other fields, Buster Crabbe is still remembered today for his serial and western portrayals on the screen.

While many of the younger generation consider his cinematic exploits as camp, Buster can take pride in knowing that Al St. John and PRC aside, his older fans still consider him a sterling example of the western hero, and while time has not been so considerate to us as it has to Buster, the mention of his name sends our memories reeling back over the years to a happier time when our hero stood toe to toe and slugged it out with the likes of Charles King and Jack Ingram.

Al St. John provided comedy relief for the somber Crabbe in his PRC westerns like **Ghost of Hidden Valley** (1946).

Buster spent a lot of time wearing ropes in scenes like this one from **His Brother's Ghost** (1946). Veteran villains Charles King and Bud Osborne flank the outlaw band.

Maxine Leslie had the drop on Buster as one-time star Kermit Maynard
handles the rope in **Raiders of Red Rock** (1947).

Jack Ingram and Buster in **Frontier Fighters** (1945).

Devil Riders (1943).

Al St. John holds Kermit Maynard at bay as Buster roughs up Stanford Jolley in **Prairie Rustlers** (1945).

Buster had Jack O'Shea where he wanted him in **Overland Riders** (1946). Crabbe's muscular physique and trim condition throughout his career made him one of the best action stars.

William Elliott

THE RETIREMENT OF WILLIAM S. HART FROM THE SCREEN IN 1925 signalled the end of realism in the silent western. Hart's stock-in-trade for a decade finally succumbed to the glossy showmanship of Tom Mix and his host of imitators. Of the western stars who rode the silent sagebrush, only Hart and Harry Carey had withstood the growing trend toward artificial glamor, which permeated the western after World War I. Both actors had painted a stark, grim and unyielding West, while portraying complex characters whose internal struggles with good and evil made them far more human than those essayed by Fred Thomson, Ken Maynard and Hoot Gibson, although there was something to be said for the sterling qualities of these heroes.

The thirties and the Depression brought a new breed of cowboy to the celluloid range; like Tom Mix, he avoided hard drink, never swore and seldom lusted after women. On occasion, he was likely to burst into song for no apparent reason and seldom lost a fight, even when the odds were overwhelming. Most were impeccable in their manners and ethics, and predictably boring. In the rush toward conformity which caught up many of the superheroes of early talkie westerns, the mantle of William S. Hart remained vacant.

The heirs to Hart's throne did not appear until after World War II, and in some respects the first was a most unlikely one. A native of Pattonsburg, Missouri, named Gordon Nance Elliott, he was educated in Kansas City, where he learned the rudimentary arts of the West at an early age. After arriving in Hollywood shortly upon completion of high school, Elliott had enrolled in the Pasadena Com-

Wild Bill Elliott.

munity Playhouse and made the leap from the stage to the movies in the late twenties, playing society roles in a screen career which thereafter remained static year after year. There seemed to be no ups or downs until he was cast as the villain in a series of Dick Foran westerns. But the real break came after more than a decade in pictures, when Gordon Elliott was cast as the lead in Columbia's *The Great Adventures of Wild Bill Hickok,* a 1938 serial which suddenly brought his career to life.

Featured as Wild Bill Saunders in his early westerns, Elliott's pictures were solid but unoriginal in their approach and story lines. Yet Bill was a distinctive change from the yodeling and singing cowboys who had flooded the western screen and his almost anemically slender figure gave Elliott a hungry appearance, which was accentuated by a thin face, hawk-like nose and flashing eyes. A distinctively different voice characterized his clipped speech and while it was seldom that Bill had very much to say, when he did, you knew that it was either a threat or a promise on which he'd make good, despite the lack of conviction in his low voice. There was also a touch of the eternal wanderer in Bill's ruggedly handsome face that was unmatched by most of the western heroes, who by and large were *too* good looking; and when he faced the villains in a showdown, everyone watching felt him completely capable of finishing anything he started.

Bill's western garb was simple and almost crude by comparison to the flashy threads worn by Gene Autry and some of the other showy dressers, yet his clothes were utilitarian in the Hart tradition. His one concession to style came late in his career—the tall hat with its brim appropriately turned up on both sides. But Bill's trademark and the touch that set him forever apart from the other gunslingers who rode the western range was a brace of six-shooters strapped handily to his side, close to the belt line. Unlike other sagebrush stars, Elliott wore his guns reversed, with the handles out for a crossdraw the likes of which no other celluloid cowboy could match. As kids in the popcorn audience, we never could understand how Wild Bill was able to draw those guns so smartly and fast in response to a challenge—it never worked that well for us despite hours of practice with our cap pistols.

Elliott inherited the role of Red Ryder, Fred Harmon's comic strip hero, from Donald Barry and while he wasn't very effective mouthing the banal dialogue required by the role of a mature adult whose sole companion for long periods of time on the trail was an Indian boy, the 16 *Ryder* films were popular. But when he left the series for Allan Lane to handle, no one was more relieved than Elliott; he was then able to experiment and develop a variety of character traits which fans of the imaginary hero would never have tolerated. Lambert Hillyer, long an associate of Hart's, played a sizeable role in these later interpretations brought to the screen by Bill. Directing several of Elliott's better westerns earlier in his career, Hillyer had recognized what would set this particular cowboy apart from the herd. As Bill moved through the forties in western after western, more and more traces of the Hart character turned up in his portrayals.

Bill made some rather good films as the forties slipped into the fifties and it was in higher status westerns like *Waco, Fargo, In Old Sacramento* and *The Fabulous Texan* that his screen character took on its final coloration. While other western heroes were busy chasing bad men up and down the plains, Elliott was not above playing the outlaw himself, with reformation a central part of the theme as long as it worked out to his own advantage, as exemplified by the role of "Spanish Jack" in *In Old Sacramento*. Bill's code of ethics was an interesting contrast to that of Autry, Rogers and Johnny Mack Brown; while an Elliott brawl was always a darn good one, the fact that his opponent was on the floor didn't prevent him from administering a suitably placed kick to finish the fight quickly. And if he needed information, Bill wasn't above disarming the villain and beating the truth from him while holding a gun on the cur. Lesser heroes would have thrashed it out on equal footing without the protection of a gun, but Bill's method was sure-fire and much more realistic.

These latter films still found Bill modest in his heroism but when the victim of a savage attack (as in *Fargo*, when he was wrapped in his own barbed wire), single-minded in a desire for revenge. Branded an outlaw because of a gunfight in *Waco*, he joined a renegade band until circumstances brought him back to the side of the law as a gunslinger-turned-peace officer. Where Rocky Lane or Johnny Mack Brown would have rounded up the old gang as their first official act, Bill went out of his way to avoid locking up the one man who had helped him, as long as he and his outlaws rode clear out of town. The end, of course, made it impossible for Bill to carry out this bargain but even as the outlaw leader was dying, he saved Bill's life—a touch of camaraderie seldom found in the B western and one that lent an additional touch.

Elliott was fortunate enough to have had a thoroughly professional and highly competent technical crew supporting his career, especially as it drew to a close. Cameraman Ernie Miller was often complimented for the pictorial beauty of his photography, especially in features like *The Fabulous Texan*, which was done in Trucolor, and provided editor Sam Fields with sufficient footage to cut around the lack of action in some of the slower-moving films that brought Bill's career to an end. While the star had usually done his own action sequences, he was often doubled by Jim Bannon in these last years; because of his age and the more mature roles he played, Bill's pace had slowed considerably and he lost more fights than he won in these final days, usually reserving gunplay for the final reel after all else had failed.

Retiring from the screen in 1954 as the program western faded into history, Wild Bill Elliott was the victim of cancer, which laid him to rest November 26, 1965. The small fry who attended Saturday matinees recognized that Bill Elliott was quite a bit different from the usual cowboy hero to whom they were accustomed, but none had ever heard of Bill Hart and realism was a factor with which they were neither acquainted nor concerned. But it's easy to understand how adults like my father, who sneered at the singing cowpokes, could appreciate the sight of Wild Bill as he parted the saloon doors, walked to the bar and belted a stiff one before searching out the man responsible for his brother's death—it was just as they might have done it.

Bill Elliott as Red Ryder in **Cheyenne Wildcat** (1944). That's Keene Duncan behind bars.

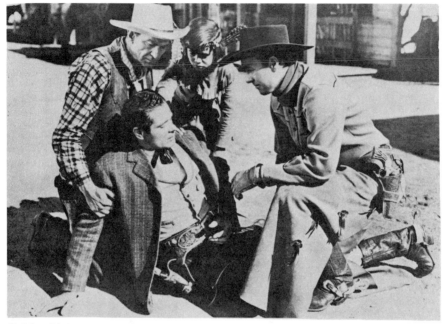

Bobby Blake played Little Beaver in the **Red Ryder** series. This is **San Antonio Kid** (1944).

Bob Steele and Alice Fleming thank Bill and his pal at the close of **Sheriff of Redwood Valley** (1946).

Bob Steele, whose career dated back to the early twenties, often faced Elliott's guns and the resulting shoot-out was always worth seeing. Steele became a past master at stealing the scene with his agonizing death act.

Bill rides with John Carroll in **The Fabulous Texan** (1947).

An exciting scene from **The Last Bandit** (1949).

Sheriff Andy Devine and Jack Holt want an explanation from Bill and Adrian Booth in **The Last Bandit.**

Bob Kent, Elliott and Ray Walker in **Rebel City** (1953).

Bill's going to get to the truth one way or another in **Beyond the Sacramento** (1941). Not the tightly clenched lips—that was his way of expressing determination.

Vera Ralston wants no part of our hero in **The Plainsman and the Lady** (1946).

Kirby Grant

CAN YOU IMAGINE EVEN A MODERATELY SUCCESSFUL BAND LEADER, especially one with his own radio show, giving it all up for a career in motion pictures? That's exactly what Kirby Grant did. A musical prodigy of sorts, this Butte, Montana, boy had capped his education with a stay at the American Conservatory of Music, then spent a couple of years in the field of classical music before organizing his own dance band and touring the country until landing a radio show in 1937. Two years later, he won a talent contest and a six-month contract at RKO, where he appeared in a series of low-budget musicals as Robert Stanton. A role in *Red River Range* (1941) introduced him to westerns, but Kirby interrupted his movie career with service in the Army until 1944.

When Rod Cameron was elevated to better roles at Universal, Grant was hired to fill in the program western slot that Cameron had vacated. His stay at Universal was less than memorable, with routine oaters predictably scripted, unimaginatively produced and marketed without a great deal of enthusiasm by the Universal sales force. There really wasn't much to be said for these westerns; Kirby appeared a bit on the heavy side and never seemed quite able to establish a heroic image in the eyes of the matinee audiences, regardless of how his fists flew or his guns blazed. The days of the good Universal westerns had ended with Johnny Mack Brown's departure for Monogram.

Monogram, whose pictures had always been considered of the basement variety—compared to those of Universal and Republic—was

103

Kirby Grant and Fuzzy Knight in **Rustlers' Roundup** (1946).

in the process of reconstructing an image, and with the acquisition of Brown, had taken a long step down a difficult road. In those days, the Monogram lot had that "We're number two, but we're going to be number one" attitude that goes a long way in making the same amount of money bring in a better product. Kirby Grant eventually turned up to lend a hand.

Cast in a series of Royal Canadian Mounted Police stories based loosely upon the works of James Oliver Curwood, Grant was given a co-star in the form of Chinook, a canine who proved to be a strong box-office draw in its own right. Kirby had many things going in his favor this time—the dog, fairly good stories reputedly from the pen of a well-known and popular author, a different background with the irresistible lure of the Mountie, who by legend always "got his man," and production values above the usual for Monogram.

Instead of claim jumpers, the crooks were now fur thieves and the villainous lawyer became an equally no-good trading post factor. Rustlers became smugglers and the Texas Rangers seemed to have donned an RCMP uniform, but it was all great fun and Kirby delivered the goods. All in all, his RCMP pictures proved a decided and refreshing change from the routine oaters issued from the B western mills, while featuring the same hard riding and straight shooting in a different guise.

But even with Northwoods pictures for Allied Artists, it couldn't last forever, and in 1954 Grant looked to the future with a keen eye; television was backoning and Kirby made the transition from Mountie to airborne Texas Ranger two years later in *Sky King*, a weekly video translation of a popular radio serial for the kids and one that found him combatting the forces of evil with an airplane instead of a horse. While *Sky King* was immensely popular for a few seasons, increasing costs eventually caught up with those early western tv series as they had with the program western and Kirby's career came to a premature close. But along with his theatrical westerns, *Sky King* can occasionally be seen on the smaller independent tv outlets across the country and Kirby Grant rides (or flies) again.

Kirby leads the fight in **Gunman's Code** (1946).

Grant has a word or two for the sheriff and pal in **Song of Idaho** (1948) as June Vincent looks on.

Kirby with Gail Davis in **Yukon Manhunt** (1951). The Mountie garb did wonders for Grant's career.

Monte Hale

ONE TRICK WHICH MOVIE STUDIOS HAD LEARNED TO KEEP THEIR TOP STARS in line—and one that had worked quite well most of the time—was to bring in an unknown and put him in starring roles, with lots of publicity and attention focused on him. After providing the necessary buildup with money and press agentry, the studio could then threaten the star that should he step out of line, the newcomer would take his place overnight with ease. In most instances where this tactic was resorted to, the recalcitrant actor took the hint, working hard to put himself back in good graces before the open threat had to be made—a not-so-subtle but highly effective maneuver on the studio's part. Occasionally the stunt backfired, as when Fox had brought Charles "Buck" Jones on the lot to keep Tom Mix under control in the twenties. While Buck Jones became a top attraction in his own right, this twist of events also benefited the studio, which stood to win either way.

With Roy Rogers feeling his oats at Republic and facing the possibility of being drafted into military service, a tall and handsome newcomer was put under contract as a possible replacement. His screen background was rather slender, but otherwise Monte Hale filled the bill. He had come to Hollywood by way of Phil Isley (Jennifer Jones's father), who had spotted Monte singing on a USO tour and the young Texan made his debut in *Stepping in Society* (1944). A natural for the western genre, Monte's accent was slight and he read lines acceptably. Although a bit on the heavy side in appearance, he was

Monte Hale.

proportioned perfectly for action, and while no Clark Gable, he did have a way with the ladies.

Rogers and Republic smoothed over their differences while Uncle Sam stood by without beckoning (although one doubts that the King of the Cowboys was seriously worried by this potential challenger) and Monte was developed into a solid second-string star with a following of his own. With his other attributes, Hale also possessed a reasonably good singing voice (after all, he'd made his living since age 12 with it) and Republic put this as well as his song writing talent to work in a series of unusual westerns; off-beat in the sense that while he was ostensibly a singing cowboy, his films were not musical westerns like those of Autry and Rogers. Instead of building the picture around the music, as had been done in the past with singing cowpokes, Monte's oaters were mainline dramas (of the melo sort) in which he stopped to sing a song now and then. In this way, he avoided the tag of singing cowboy (for those who abhorred that ilk) and yet the music was there to shorten the script and action necessary to fill out the five reels.

Monte's screen personality was a questionable point; he never projected with the strength of a Don Barry, Bill Elliott or Johnny Mack Brown. In fact, were there not so many lesser western leading men who are more deserving of the description, you could call him likeable but colorless, but other things compensated for this shortcoming, among them gorgeous leading ladies, fun-filled fisticuff free-for-alls and solid production values including the use of Trucolor, which some would prefer to call a liability as it was mainly green and orange.

Out California Way was typical of the somewhat different ideas concocted for Hale. Betty Burbridge, an experienced and quite proficient lady whose western writing credits dated back to 1925 and the days of Buffalo Bill Jr., Wally Wales and Buddy Roosevelt, put together a story that cast Monte as an aspiring movie actor who met up with young Bobby Blake and his horse. Blake's ambitions ran along parallel lines and the two tried cracking Hollywood together. John Dehner portrayed the villainous star whose popularity was threatened once Hale landed a job at the studio and Roy Rogers, Allan Lane and Don Barry all made walk-on appearances to give the story a semblance of reality while adding advertising value for exhibitors. With occasional boosts like this, Monte lasted until 1951 with Republic and was one of the final program western stars to bow out of the saddle.

Monte Hale held a rather unusual and high opinion of his own talents, the prerogative of a star, but when the end arrived and he walked off the Republic lot for the last time, the unemployed actor had the good sense not to sign with an independent as had some of his other acquaintances. He called it quits right there and embarked on a singing tour with Ray Whitley's western group, then toured with various circuses and rodeos before finally hanging up the gaudy dress for retirement.

Monte rounds up the last of the gang for sheriff Ed Cobb as lovely Adrian Booth looks on in **Last Frontier Uprising** (1947).

Roy Barcroft provides a moment of suspense for the kids as he takes careful aim at Monte's back in **Law of the Golden West** (1949).

Paul C. Hurst appeared in several of Monte's westerns. A prolific actor-director of the silent era, Hurst was equally effective as a drunken old codger or a crafty outlaw. Gail Davis would later appear as Calamity Jane in a television series.

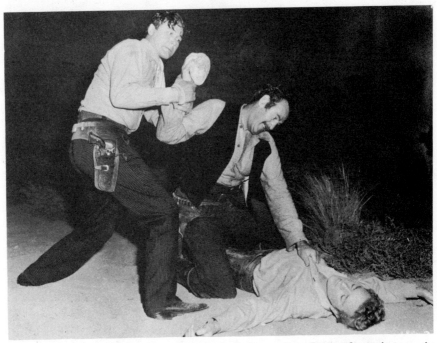

Monte was husky enough to handle villainous Roy Barcroft with ease in **The Missourians** (1950).

Under Colorado Skies (1947).

Russell Hayden

OF THE MULTITUDE OF ACTORS WHO FILLED THE SAGEBRUSH SCREEN WITH action, none came better prepared for stardom than Russell Hayden. While others relied upon their athletic prowess or vocal cords to get them by the camera successfully, Hayden could point to a solid background in virtually every aspect of moviemaking. Born Hayden Lucid in Chico, California, he had started work as a grip at Universal, then moved over to Paramount's sound department where he rose through the ranks to assistant cameraman. He even tried his hand as an agent before undertaking a few minor acting roles in 1934— all this by age 22. Three years later, he was chosen to replace James Ellison in the Hopalong Cassidy westerns and moved into the role of "Lucky Jenkins" with ease.

As Hoppy's sidekick, Ellison had been somewhat less than happy; the role had called for him to do virtually everything from romancing the young ladies to handling the villains in gun duels and fist fights. His dramatic range unfortunately didn't extend quite that far. Hayden's duties were a bit more circumscribed but there were still times when the audience had good reason to believe that he and not Bill Boyd was the real star. At any rate, he proved a fortunate addition to the series and lasted through the 1941 season before moving out on his own.

Hayden was well-versed in the histrionic requirements for western stardom, and gritting his teeth between tightly clenched lips in what became a characteristic pose for him, Russ could simulate a knock-down-dragout fight as well as any of the other program western stars.

Beginning as "Lucky" Jenkins in the Hopalong Cassidy series, Russ Hayden rose to starring role in 1940. With J. Farrell McDonald and Julie Carter in **Stagecoach War.**

His style was lean, even sparse, and ever conscious of production techniques, Hayden took pains to make his appearances as realistic as possible. His garb was as plain and unadorned as his acting style and Russ turned up next in a group of Harry Sherman's Paramount westerns, probably the best productions of his screen career.

Moving over to Columbia's corral for a couple of seasons, Hayden worked with Charles Starrett for awhile and then headed up his own series before entering the Army in 1944. The Columbia oaters featured Walter "Dub" Taylor as his sidekick and brought in the musical element with Bob Wills and his Texas Playboys, resulting in a series of routine westerns whose major interests rested in the gorgeous leading ladies (like Adele Mara and Ann Savage) for the adults in the back rows and an occasional change of scenery (as in *Riders of the Northwest Mounted*) for the kids down front. But Russ was a new face under the Columbia logo and his pictures met with considerable popularity at the time.

After discharge from the Army, Russ teamed up with Jimmy Ellison to co-produce and co-star in a series of inexpensive independents which are still exciting when seen today. There wasn't much in the way of logic or plots, but between the two stars, they kept the action rolling and Hayden's screen personality actually loosened up a bit, making him appear more human and fallible, somewhat of a departure from the days of his Columbia oaters. But the series was short-lived and Russ made a few straight-action westerns for Republic in the late forties before moving out of motion pictures completely. Quite aware of what was happening to the program western, Hayden looked for the right opportunity and moved into television production in an executive capacity.

While Russell Hayden's career as an actor and star was far from a spectacular one, he was a seasoned performer who could always be counted upon for an exciting show and his low-budget pictures often ranked among the best on the screen. For action-adventure fans, he delivered no-nonsense performances which compared quite favorably to the work Tim Holt was doing at RKO, and if we could fault him for anything, it would have to be the completely deadpan expression of mock seriousness with which he worked. But looking at some of his westerns today, one is struck by the thought that had he delivered the dialogue in any other manner, Hayden would probably have broken out in laughter at some of the lines he was required to speak. Those of us who cheered "Lucky" Hayden on to greater glory were really more interested in what he did than in what he said, and Russ gave us plenty of hard riding and straight shooting to offset the verbal interludes.

Russ took on the best of them, from Stan Ridges in **Silver on the Sage** (1939) . . .

. . . to Victor Jory in **Knights of the Range** (1940).

Russ checked the stage driver for injury while Bob Wills held the baddies at attention. That's Walter "Dub" Taylor behind the door in **The Lone Prairie** (1940).

Russ spent much of his time trying to find out who did it in **Saddles and Sagebrush** (1943). When mild threats didn't work . . .

. . . a closer look at the persuader was in order.

Russ and Bob Wills in **Riders of the Nothwest Mounted** (1943). Besides providing the musical interludes, Wills and his musical group were integral members of the cast instead of a tack-on for good measure.

Gorgeous Lynne Roberts and Russ in **Sons of Adventure** (1948). As kids, we didn't really appreciate the beauty surrounding our favorites but with hindsight, can now understand that it just might have been difficult to leave the ladies for a fistfight.

'Neath Canadian Skies.

Tim Holt

VERY FEW OF THE SILENT SCREEN'S ACTION-ADVENTURE STARS COULD POINT with pride to a son following in their celluloid footsteps, and of those who tried to emulate their famous sires, success in leading roles eluded the majority. There seemed to be much truth in the maxim that talent wasn't necessarily passed on from one generation to another, nor did the possession of a well-known surname guarantee a career. Those, like Creighton Chaney and Douglas Fairbanks Jr., who won fame managed it mainly on their own merit. Only one rose to leading roles in the western arena, creating a career that lasted almost two decades —Charles John Holt Jr., the son of Jack Holt and better known to his admirers as Tim.

Born in 1918, young Holt had received an early introduction to the screen when he played the role of his father as a child in *The Vanishing Pioneer* (1928) but a screen career did not follow. Tim completed school, attending Culver Military Academy before deciding to try his luck as an actor. Signed by Walter Wanger in 1936 for a role in *History Is Made at Night* (with Charles Boyer and Jean Arthur), young Holt went on to become one of RKO's most durable contract stars, trailing only Ginger Rogers at that studio in popularity. He also confounded reviewers and critics, who found his screen portrayals in *Stagecoach* and *The Magnificent Ambersons* most promising and could not understand why the talented youngster was content to remain a star in low-budget westerns.

Unpretentious oaters produced on a modest scale by men like Bart Gilroy, the plot ingredients of the prewar Tim Holt westerns were

Tim Holt.

both standard and familiar to all western fans, but the mixture was concocted with a skilled hand that displayed the very youthful and personable star at his best, quickly winning Tim a large following. For some time he was fortunate to enjoy the talent of Harry Wilde behind the camera, and the excellent photography of the scenic locations in these early westerns added a large plus to Tim's screen appearances, as his series replaced RKO's earlier one with George O'Brien, also a quality product.

Enlisting in the U.S. Army Air Corps in 1942, Tim spent part of his tour of duty stateside establishing training facilities. Sent to the Far East as part of a B–29 bomber crew, Holt flew 22 combat missions over Japan, barely managing to limp back to Guam on his last. Returning to RKO after discharge in 1945 as a Major, Tim resumed his career with a role in *My Darling Clementine* before moving back into his own western series. While critical acclaim came his way once again for a moving portrayal in *The Treasure of the Sierra Madre*, Tim Holt rode the range for another six years, beginning with a remake of Zane Grey's *Under the Tonto Rim,* in which he played a stage line operator who passed himself off as an outlaw to find the men responsible for his best friend's death. This proved to be the usual western corn but packaged in a glossy production, and Tim drew considerable notice among exhibitors. In hopes of broadening his appeal among the young audiences, Holt acquired a sidekick in the person of Richard Martin, who was given the role of an Irish-Mexican named Chito. During these years, Tim also bought into the Lamarr & Jennings Rodeo in Norman, Oklahoma, reorganizing it as the Tim Holt–Lamarr & Jennings Rodeo and touring as its star during the off-season.

Developing gradually as the star had matured, Holt's screen character was a likable one but he was quite often tight-lipped and this taciturnity left much of the dialogue as well as comedy to Chito, whose good-natured jesting reflected that of an over-aged and temporarily reformed juvenile delinquent. Tim's romantic interludes with his leading ladies (usually Jane Nigh, Joan Dixon or Dorothy Malone) were businesslike and not particularly convincing, as he always seemed anxious to get on with the business at hand. But to those of us in the matinee audience, it all seemed natural enough; at least Tim didn't sing to the ladies. We could easily identify with a hero who preferred action to romance and our own adolescent confusion over the battle of the sexes produced a similar response—let's get on with the action! Except for a pair of thin leather gloves, our hero also avoided the fancy clothes worn by other western stars and was quite often seen wearing unfashionable denims, or at best a rather plain shirt with striped trousers, which added to the realism.

Produced mainly by Herman Schlom and directed by Leslie Selander, these postwar RKO-Tim Holt westerns managed to maintain a high degree of integrity in the declining days of the program western. Selander's expert direction of well-scripted stories was accentuated by the photography, which had continued in the tradition of Harry Wilde. While other westerns fell victim to economy measures in production, including shorter scripts and fewer camera set-ups, Holt's producers resisted such, and as a result production costs zoomed to almost $100,000 each at a time when the competition was spending less on their product. While this made Tim's films look very good by comparison, the box-office returns unfortunately did not increase and so with *The Marshal of Pecos* in 1952, Tim Holt rode off into the sunset for the final time.

After leaving RKO, Tim's immediate plans had included a TV series which would have carried on the adventures of his RKO unit for the small screen, but this prospect was never successfully developed; Tim appeared in a few low-budget thrillers and then retired from the screen. Although he's put on a bit of weight over the years, Tim still retains his youthful appearance and now lives in Oklahoma with his third wife, where he works as the sales manager of a radio station. Looking back at his screen career, Tim views his films with pride (as he should) and agrees with those who mourn the passing of the B western and its heroes. Understanding the audience's needs to identify with the leading characters, Tim Holt finds it difficult to believe that today's fans can do so with the current western stars and he's right. Perhaps the emphasis on justice, fair play and an invincible hero was overdone at times in the low-budget westerns, but what parent wants his youngsters to identify with sex, violence and deceit? Not Tim or the others who would like to see heroes on the order of their generation revived.

Tim won critical acclaim for his role in John Ford's **Stagecoach** (1939).

Robbers of the Range (1941) featured this hard-riding scene.

Holt's post-war westerns paired him with Richard Martin. From **Hot Lead** (1951).

Better remembered as Tom Keene, Dick Powers (r) is in for a workout in **Wild Horse Mesa** (1948).

Under the Tonto Rim (1947).

With lovely ladies like Joan Dixon cluttering up Tim's pictures, it's a wonder he could find time to enforce **The Law of the Badlands** (1950).

With Lois Martin in **Outlaw Valley.**

Determined to put all crooked bankers out of business, the heroine is hidden under that mask, but she'll get help from Tim in **Masked Raiders** (1949).

A time-worn rescue western style, in **Border Treasure** (1950), with Jane Nigh. It would have been interesting (and different) if just for once the wagon had outrun the hero.

Mauritz Hugo is about to teach Tim a lesson in **Saddle Legion** (1950).

With James Bush in **Saddle Legion.** Tim was the rare western hero who smoked on-screen.

George Houston

THE COMING OF SOUND THREW THE ENTIRE MOTION PICTURE INDUSTRY into a maelstrom of self-doubt and even the Warner Brothers, who had forced the revolution with their Vitaphone, were not quite certain exactly where it would all lead. During the latter twenties, the art of the silent screen had developed to a high degree, leaving only westerns and cheap melodrama for the Poverty Row producers, who had neither the funds nor the inclination to emulate the deMilles, Lloyds or Ingrams on the other side of the tracks.

Actually, the economics of independent production had been very good for the shrewd producer able to sell the product grinding through his cameras in the early twenties, but a general slump in box-office business in mid decade had started to tilt the picture in the opposite direction. Major studios had virtually abdicated the western range, with the exception of the Mix and Jones features for Fox and Tim McCoy's adventures at M-G-M, and the independents quickly rushed in to fill the void. Westerns were by comparison inexpensive to produce and attracted a wide audience. Yet the advent of the talkies nearly destroyed the genre and it wasn't until 1929 that sufficient technical advances in sound recording and reproduction allowed the incorporation of the one element of realism that the silent western lacked. Henry McRae at Universal and Leo Maloney in the independent field each demonstrated the feasibility of talking westerns; one with a sagebrush serial (*The Indians Are Coming*), the other with a feature, *Overland Bound*. While both were rather primitive in conception and execution, they proved a point; and independent film

134

George Houston.

makers returned to the western with a vengeance, flooding the screen during the thirties with so many series that compiling them presents a major problem.

Of the independent companies, few enjoyed as much success with as little talent as did Producers Releasing Corporation (PRC), the brainchild of Henry Briggs and Leon Fromkiss which made its debut in 1940 with 12 releases. Financed on the proverbial shoestring common to such ventures, it lasted nearly a decade. During those years it set what must be some kind of record, as at one time or another it featured the talents of a vast assortment of tumbleweed troupers, including Buster Crabbe, Eddie Dean, Al LaRue, Bob Livingston, Tim McCoy, Jim Newill, Dave O'Brien, Tex Ritter and Bob Steele. While critics were content to sneer at PRC westerns, audiences (especially kids) ate up the predictable plots, routine action and familiar casts which were as much a trademark as the PRC logo.

One of its more interesting series characters appeared in 1941—Bob Livingston's "The Lone Rider." Livington's contribution had been the development of a no-nonsense troubleshooter who rode the range righting the multitude of wrongs which plagued the cinematic West, but when he and PRC came to a parting of the ways in 1943, the Lone Rider was to be gracefully retired from the screen, or so it was believed. Enter George Houston.

Houston had enjoyed a rather mediocre film career after turning to acting in 1934 with a role in *The Melody Lingers On;* he had been much more successful as a singer. A graduate of Rutgers and the Juilliard Institute of Music, George had joined the Navy during World War I, and after his discharge he eventually opened his own vocal studio, offering to teach others how to sing. This modestly unprofitable venture was abandoned for a lack of students and he landed a position with New York's American Opera Company, but classical music soon went the same route, and Houston moved to the Broadway stage where he found some fame in *Shooting Star, New Moon* and *Thumbs Up.* From Broadway, it was only a short jump to the screen; but Houston found himself in an entirely new arena—playing an entirely new game—after making the move. For the first time, George found himself surrounded by song and dance men, all eager to advance their own career at the next guy's expense. After several years of shuffling nowhere, he decided to make the move into the saddle.

Houston talked about keeping the Lone Rider. PRC listened and accepted. So the Lone Rider reappeared with Houston portraying the dauntless hero, although the characterization was altered from Livingston's austere portrayal to one of a good-natured singing cowboy; for some readers, that should say enough.

But George's Lone Rider wasn't cut from the same cloth as the plethora of cactus crooners; Houston projected as a hard-riding and rightly feared champion of justice who occasionally let his hair down long enough to belt out a ballad over the prairie. Standing well over six feet and favoring the flat-crowned Stetson which gave him an imposing appearance on screen, George Houston presented a rather awesome figure. Looking just a bit like the Stewart Granger of several years later, this new Lone Rider was a decided change for the better, as singing cowboys went, and presaged a trend which others would soon adopt—an emphasis on action instead of song with the incidental music becoming a positive factor in his films instead of the detraction it presented in other western series.

Unfortunately, George Houston and the Lone Rider lasted but a short two years before PRC abandoned the series and character completely and Houston died. Some have placed the blame on poor box-office returns; others at the public's dismay with yet another yodeling gunslinger, but in reality, PRC and other independents were among the first to feel the financial death blow that would eventually strike down every program western in the early fifties. PRC could not make and sell its product cheaply enough to undercut rentals on better westerns like the Tim Holt and Johnny Mack Brown oaters, nor were their stars sufficiently popular to outdraw Gene Autry and Roy Rogers at the end. And so George Houston and the Lone Rider passed into an early and undeserved obscurity, with the man who had such a brief fling at screen fame meeting with an untimely death in 1945 at age 47.

Outlaws of Boulder Pass (1943).

What a way to go! **Frontier Fury** (1944).

Houston was a match for any crook, especially if he chose to sing them to death.

Once George reveals that he's The Lone Rider, **The Border Roundup**
(1943) will end.

Tom Keene

THE B WESTERN HAD MORE THAN ITS SHARE OF FRUSTRATED DRAMATIC actors, many of whom had turned to the outdoor adventure epic with hopes that a so-so career would suddenly catch fire, burning up the celluloid prairie in a roaring flame of popularity. When making this move, they usually acquired a new name, or at least a nickname, to match the action image; and so it was with George Duryea, whose work on the stage had led him to the early sound screen with a starring role in Cecil B. deMille's *The Godless Girl,* a partial talkie of 1929. Several other solid roles followed this debut, but nothing much seemed to come as a result. The competition in straight dramatic acting was heavy and so Duryea changed his name to Tom Keene, accepting an RKO-Pathé contract to star in a western series. As Keene, he made a dozen above-average oaters for RKO between 1931 and 1933, and a career that had been heading nowhere in particular suddenly took on new life.

While his next move may have been a soul-satisfying one to him personally, it was hardly wise. Determined to avoid being typed as a strictly western star, Keene left Hollywood for summer stock, and when he returned six months later to undertake a role in King Vidor's *Our Daily Bread,* everything had gone as he planned it; no one remembered the dashing young man. Dramatic leads were mixed with starring roles in Paramount westerns and the two kept body and soul together until 1936, when he was signed by E. B. Derr to essay the lead in a series of historical dramas for Crescent Pictures. Eight such films followed, each based upon specific historical incidents as the

George Duryea, alias Tom Keene, alias Richard Powers.

Bozeman Massacre (*The Glory Trail*) and the discovery of silver in Virginia City (*Battle of Greed*). His leading lady in two of the series was a fiery Latin working under the name Rita Casino; a decade later her fame as Rita Hayworth saw opportunists retitle and reissue both pictures with starring credit shifted from Keene to Rita.

Realizing that playing western leads was not such a bad way to earn a living, Keene temporarily convinced himself that sagebrush fame was preferable to none at all, and for the next five years he worked quite regularly for Monogram; but late in 1942, the frustrated thespian in him succumbed to the urge once more, and leaving the screen again he joined a stage play heading for Broadway, where he changed his name to Richard Powers. The play bombed rather badly, but Duryea-Keene-Powers received kind words from reviewers for his histrionic efforts.

However kind reviews do not necessarily fill an empty stomach and he returned to Hollywood again, where he did a few leading but non-western parts as Powers and a large number of character roles for RKO until 1950. That year, he turned up at Republic again, guesting in Roy Rogers's *Trail of Robin Hood,* and as Richard Powers, he played the lead in a 12-chapter western cliffhanger, *Desperadoes of the West.* But the starring career was largely over, as was the confusion over his name. Settling into the comfortable rut he had tried so long and hard to avoid, our man of many names was seen in a number of television westerns before retiring to devote his time and energy to real estate and insurance.

Tom Keene missed stardom by several leagues and for as many reasons. A fairly competent character actor, he couldn't seem to consistently project the authority that a western hero needed. There seemed nothing distinctive about his appearance, personality or the roles he played—a handicap that might have been overcome with a mystery identity or some other gimmick. But mostly, his heart wasn't really in the saddle, and he accepted his screen career as a westerner and man of action mainly because the long-sought dramatic career failed to materialize. An imaginative producer might have come up with the answer; other fairly colorless personalities before (and after) him were successful in translating mediocre histrionic talents into fame and fortune. Yet Tom Keene had his fame, and looking back from the vantage point of four decades, he appears to be the one who missed the boat ride to success while searching for a rocket going the same way.

With Sally Starr in **Pardon My Gun** (1930).

The Sundown Trail (1931).

Tom and Bobby Nelson in **Partners** (1932).

Caught by surprise, Tom was overpowered in **Ghost Valley** (1932). It happened in every oater.

With Billy Butts and Yakima Canutt in **Scarlet River** (1933).

Buster Crabbe may have had the lead in **Drift Fence** (1936), but Keene had Katherine De Mille.

After slugging it out in **Dynamite Canyon** (1941) with Keene Dun
can . . .

. . . Tom deserved this moment of relaxation in **Western Mail** (1942).
Frank Yaconelli's on strings.

No self-respecting western hero would have let sheriff Glenn Strange just walk up and take his six-shooter. Could it have been the coffee or Eleanor Stewart's eyes that did it? From **The Painted Trail** (1938).

Tom closed out his career with character and supporting roles under the name Richard Powers. This is from Tim Holt's **Wild Horse Mesa** (1948).

Allan Lane

IT ALMOST SEEMS THAT TO BECOME A B WESTERN STAR, ONE HAD TO HAVE a college degree complete with pigskin heroics in his background. While this is something of an overstatement, a surprising number of actors who rose to fame in the saddle had exactly that—John Wayne, Charles Starrett, Johnny Mack Brown and Harry Albershart, the latter more easily recognized by his fans as Allan "Rocky" Lane. But unlike the others, Lane did not travel directly from the gridiron to the screen.

Born in Mishawaka, Indiana, he attended Notre Dame, winning varsity letters in football, baseball, and basketball, but Lane left college before graduating to join the National Players, a Cincinnati theatrical stock company. A road company presenting *Hit the Deck* arrived in the city without its leading man and with less than a year's experience in the theatre, the young athlete-actor joined the road show and finished the tour, reaching New York at the season's close. Once there, Lane had decided to make the stage his career and eventually found work in several Broadway plays.

During this time he became interested in photography, and between plays, he formed his own company, which specialized in commercial photography. Lane spent four years building the business into a well-known studio with Ford Motors, Wrigley's chewing gum, Camay soap and Lucky Strike cigarettes numbered among his clients. However he closed shop after having been discovered by a Fox talent scout. To this point, Lane's career sounds as if doors simply opened for him, but there was much hard work involved and a long road left to travel. Hollywood (like television after it) was an enormous con-

Allan Lane.

Add a stetson and change of shirt—presto! Rocky Lane.

sumer of talent at the time and it was entirely possible to be a credit-
able performer with a static career. For ten years between 1929 and
1938, this was the case with Allan Lane. As a Fox contract player, his
roles in films like *Sing and Be Happy*, *The Jones Family in Big Business* and *Fifty Roads to Town* were all enjoyable, but while one led
to another, none seemed to lead upward to real fame.

Eventually leaving Fox, Lane moved to RKO, and in 1938 he
appeared on the screen in his first leading role; the picture was *Night
Spot* and was followed by *Maid's Night Out* with Joan Fontaine. But
starring roles at RKO were not necessarily the top step in the business
and like so many others before (and after) him, Lane realized that
juvenile roles would not last forever, nor would they continue to keep
him in the public eye for long. Accordingly, he joined Republic's roster
of action-adventure stars, and after the required serial role (*King of
the Royal Mounted*, 1939), he found himself sitting in a saddle answer-
ing to the nickname "Rocky."

It was an unusual choice for the actor; the slender 185-pound six-
footer was a well-proportioned hero, but somehow Allan Lane never
managed to project himself confidently as a western star. Perhaps
it was the gloves he wore or the rather fastidious manner in which he
toyed with them, but somehow Rocky always seemed to be just a bit
of the dandy. But looks were deceiving and this apparently helped to
account for his popularity, for Lane could stage an excellent if exag-
gerated brawl, and time and again he brought villainous Roy Barcroft
to his knees with scythe-like haymaker punches that cut swaths
through the air. Of course, all of us sitting in the audience really believed the fights to be real, but looking back now, it would have been
interesting to see just how Rocky and some of Republic's other western
heroes would have stacked up in an actual duel of fists; at least on
celluloid they were all winners.

Lane worked steadily in westerns for Republic, but his big chance
arrived in 1945, when he fell heir to the *Red Ryder* series. Bill Elliott
had vacated the role for better things and Rocky became the third
actor to portray the fictional hero. The first of 21 Lane *Red Ryder*
adventures, *Stage Coach to Denver*, appeared in 1946; Bobby Blake
continued as Little Beaver and Emmett Lynn came on as Lane's sidekick. This opener was a variation of the hoary land-grab plot but it
featured more hard riding, fist fights and high-speed coach driving
than plot, making Lane's claim to the role secure. Strangely enough,
he was the most popular of the actors who portrayed the comic strip
redhead, yet Don "Red" Barry had given the best performances and

Jim Bannon (who followed Lane as the fourth Ryder) came the closest to filling the physical requirements with which Fred Harmon had endowed his hero.

Rocky's *Red Ryder* westerns suffered to some extent from the same affliction that had made Bill Elliott's tenure in the role so unbearable for him; the banal dialogue scripted between the Indian youngster and the adult cowpoke had been painfully delivered by Wild Bill, and so the writers cut back on the lengthy and sometimes ridiculous conversations; yet somehow Lane managed to make it all sound more believable no matter how badly it was written. I suppose one of the reasons we enjoyed Rocky so much was this very sincerity; regardless of the scene or circumstances, he came across as being deadly earnest (without dropping into parody) and with colorfully titled sagas like *Carson City Raiders, The Silver City Kid, Death Valley Gunfighters* and *Night Riders of Monterey,* he lasted until the B western's end in 1954.

Unlike some of the other sagebrush heroes, Allan Lane did not have to suffer the indignity of character roles and bit parts for a living. He did public appearance tours for two years while still fresh in the youngsters' minds and after a few supporting roles on television, became the voice for the talking horse (Mr. Ed) that made a shambles of Alan Young's life for several seasons before going into reruns. His feature westerns had almost without variance run remarkably true to a slender formula—Tom London and Roy Barcroft turned up in nearly every one and the appearance of old Tom (who had enjoyed a starring career of his own in the silents as Leonard Clapham) became a ritual which those of us who appreciated good acting as we grew older especially enjoyed.

Lane had the advantage of good supporting actors, no musical sequences and plenty of footage employing Republic's talented action experts; and despite the fact that to the bitter end he still sounded suspiciously like an Eastern dude and not the undercover lawman he claimed to be, we all loved him for it. In retirement today, he can look back on a career that gave a generation lots of clean thrills and excitement, yet I'd still swear that the stranger in town was really a tenderfoot and not Red Ryder.

Sheriff Tom London breaks up a brawl between Lane and Roy Barcroft as Max Terhune and Duncan Renaldo look on in **Sheriff of Sundown** (1944).

Emmett Lynn and Lane in **Stagecoach to Denver** (1946), first of his **Red Ryder** series.

Rocky hit equally hard with either fist; a left in **Bandit King of Texas** (1949) . . .

. . . and a right in **Salt Lake Raiders** (1950).

ike the mounts of all sagebrush heroes, Allan's horse had a name and
ersonality of its own. This is Black Jack and master in action from
owder River Rustlers (1949).

Desert of Lost Men (1951).

With Eddie Waller and Bob Steele in **Savage Frontier** (1953).

"You tell your boss"—Bob Wilke doesn't believe it, but Lane's going to put the **Corpus Christi Bandits** (1945) behind bars and Tom London just may lend a hand.

Lash LaRue

NO MATTER HOW YOU SLICE THE CAKE, CUT THE MUSTARD, CHOP THE
wood or crush the ice, there never was a more unlikely western hero
than one Alfred LaRue, a Gretna, Louisiana, boy who disguised his
real identity on the screen for a few years under the alias of Lash
LaRue. A graduate of College of the Pacific in Stockton, California,
who had tried his hand at salesmanship (real estate) until the acting
bug bit him, Al certainly must have been the butt of many "Would
you buy a used car from this man?" sort of jokes. It's not that he was
really dishonest or anything of that sort, but young LaRue had a sulky,
downright mean look about him (about which he could do nothing)
and even his broadest smile reminded you of a Prohibition racketeer
who had just heard that his crosstown rival had turned up in con-
crete shoes.

Enjoying very little luck in his early attempts to crack Hollywood's
golden gates, LaRue seemed to be traveling a nowhere road when a
role in Universal's 1946 cliffhanger *The Master Key* (starring Milburn
Stone later of *Gunsmoke* fame) led to one in PRC's *Song of Old Wyoming* (1945), an Eddie Dean oater filmed in Cinecolor. As the dashing
Cheyenne Kid, Al was perfect; his villainous appearance was accentuated by a resemblance to Humphrey Bogart and a strange walk,
all of which added flavor to his portrayal of a hired gun imported to
break poor old Ma Conway by running off her cattle and gunning
down her ranch hands, allowing the chief villains to acquire her land.
As the plot moved merrily along, the Kid suddenly discovered that he
was old Ma's missing son, and repenting his loathsome ways, switched

159

Run! It's Lash LaRue, Scourge of the West, in **Dead Man's Gold** (1949).

sides only to die at the end. Garbed completely in black from flat crown Stetson to his boots, Al LaRue was the epitome of evil and it was this role which created his starring career; Jack Palance was launched to fame via the same route in *Shane* a few years later.

It has been reported that PRC received so much mail concerning LaRue's portrayal of the Cheyenne Kid that the character was revived in a spinoff series, but others credit substantial investments made to help PRC with its perennial financing problems as the magic sesame that opened the doors for Al. How it happened is really immaterial; suffice it to say that one of the program western's more effective looking villains suddenly became a hero. His use of the distinctive black outfit (which included his horse) broke with tradition, which had always reserved black for the bad guys; Charles Starrett's Durango Kid was a mystery character wanted by the law and remains the sole exception of importance to this rule. LaRue reappeared on the screen teamed with Al St. John, riding through a series of Cheyenne Kid adventures (*Return of Cheyenne, Cheyenne Rides Again, Cheyenne*

Takes Over), many of which were better than the average PRC western.

Somewhere along the way, Al developed a knack for cracking a bullwhip, and when the PRC series was completed, he moved over to Eagle-Lion and then Screen Guild as Lash LaRue (*The Lash, Return of the Lash, Law of the Lash*). Armed with two guns and a whip with which he could do simple stunts, LaRue continued his western heroism. With the assistance of stock footage and a double for the hard-riding active scenes (Al wasn't much of a horseman), he created a minor sort of legend among western fans that even today brings him to mind before Whip Wilson, a far better rider and whip expert, is recalled.

Part of the legend revolved around the emphasis on black which surrounded this unusual hero. While Whip Wilson looked like the good guy, there was nothing outstanding about him or his screen personality. At least, in his black garb Lash kept your eye constantly focused on him. Once you could accept LaRue as the hero, along with the bullwhip and his heavy use of the two handy six-shooters, there was a comfortable feeling about the whole thing—you knew that no villain could possibly prove a match for anyone with as mean a look in his eye as good old Lash LaRue.

But no matter how good the gimmick it couldn't last forever, and by 1950 Lash's starring career was ending. He dropped back to supporting and character roles before leaving the screen for what seemed to be the required circus tours and then briefly hosting a television show (which played reruns of his pictures) before dropping into retirement and out of sight. But any way you look at it, he left his mark on the program western—who could forget that name?

Al LaRue rode with Roscoe Ates in his PRC series as "The Cheyenne Kid."

Roscoe Ates, Al LaRue and Eddie Dean in **Wild West** (1946).

After a disappointing career, LaRue rose to stardom with his portrayal of The Cheyenne Kid in Eddie Dean's **Song of Old Wyoming** (1945). Here he has baddies Ian Keith and Robert Barron in his sights.

Hired to run Sarah Padden off her land, LaRue learned that he was really her son. Horace Murphy looks on in **Song of Old Wyoming.**

Eddie Dean's oaters weren't noted for much, but **Song of Old Wyoming**
did introduce Al LaRue as a new western hero. With Sarah Padden,
Emmett Lynn, Dean and Jennifer Holt.

George O'Brien

"HE'S NOT A CAVEMAN OR A LOUNGE LIZARD—HE'S A MAN'S MAN AND an idol of women!" Thus read the advertisements for George O'Brien's first starring role in John Ford's 1924 *The Iron Horse*. Like so many other motion picture personalities, O'Brien had spent many years working to become the overnight sensation which the role of Davy Brandon had brought to him.

The son of San Francisco policeman (later Chief of Police) David O'Brien, George was born in 1900. Learning to ride and rope on a ranch near Los Gatos, he mastered football, baseball, track and swimming while attending Polytechnic High School. Looking and acting in real life like the Irishman he was, George donned Navy blues for two years in 1917, after convincing the elder O'Brien to sign his enlistment papers; and while in uniform he tackled boxing, winning the light-heavyweight title of the Pacific fleet.

Discharged in 1919, George planned to study medicine but a chance meeting with Tom Mix altered his plans forever. Mix was shooting on location near San Francisco, and wherever he went America's Champion Cowboy made it a point to look up the local law enforcement officials, trading stories of the good old days (Mix had been a lawman years before). George's father suggested that Mix might take his son back to Hollywood when he returned and so George O'Brien became an assistant cameraman, lugging 90 pounds of movie camera around the Mix lot for almost two years before deciding to return to school.

Back in San Francisco, George met Lambert Hillyer, who hired him

George O'Brien came to stardom in John Ford's **The Iron Horse** (1924).
Here he is with Warren Hymer and Sue Carol in **Lone Star Ranger**
(1930).

as a bit player and stuntman; one of his typical parts at this time
called for the athletic youngster to swim underwater with a fake
shark fin tied to his back. Hearing studio scuttlebutt that an unknown
was being sought for the role of Davy in *The Iron Horse*, he returned
to Hollywood where he managed to test for the part. The resulting
six-month contract called for $125 weekly and release of the film
brought him instant stardom. Elated, Fox quickly rushed their new
find into two more pictures with Dorothy Mackaill, and O'Brien went
on to demonstrate his versatility in both western and non-western
roles, winning popular acclaim for roles in *Three Badmen*, *Sunrise*
(with Janet Gaynor) and *Noah's Ark*, made on loan-out to Warners.
His first talkie in 1929 (*Salute*) also contained John Wayne and Ward

Bond, two actors who would soon become almost totally identified with the western genre.

Many of O'Brien's westerns at this time were adapted from Zane Grey stories (*The Lone Star Ranger, Last of the Duanes, Riders of the Purple Sage*), and Fox provided him with good writers, skillful directors and very competent supporting casts, elevating his sagebrush appearances far above the potboiler formula western format. A rugged son of Erin, O'Brien was perfectly cast in the Zane Grey pictures and possessed sufficient acting ability to bring his roles to life. Where the quickie westerns were shot in five to seven days, the Fox O'Brien westerns took as much as seven weeks, with much location shooting involved. In 1931, David Howard took over as George O'Brien's director with *The Rainbow Trail,* an association that lasted for several years. Many of his films introduced personalities who would later become stars in their own right: Betsy Ross King, a nine-year old rodeo stunt rider, Clair Trevor, George Beldam (better known as Rex Bell) and Joel McCrea, whose screen test was arranged by O'Brien using Dan Clark, his unit cameraman.

Clark was only one of many in the O'Brien production unit who had joined George when Tom Mix left Fox in 1929. Mix had more real cowboys on his personal payroll than any other western star, and many others on the Fox roster. Knowing the caliber of these men, George was delighted to have them working with him. Stuntmen Sid Jordan and Herman Nowlin were among the best known; Jordan had been with Mix since 1913 and Nowlin since 1924. While they performed some of O'Brien's dangerous work, George really did much of it himself. Jordan was a sharpshooter and when a bullet supposedly fired by the villain struck near the hero on-screen, it was actually a real bullet fired by Sid from behind the camera; Jordan could put a bullet in a dime time after time with ease. Dick Hunter handled the horses, and with Jordan driving a six-horse team in a sequence involving a horse-to-vehicle jump, O'Brien knew the wagon or stage would be in the right position and steady enough to make the transfer.

By 1935, Fox wanted out of the sagebrush business and O'Brien was the last westerner on its payroll. Sol Lesser, who had produced for Fox, was now at RKO and in the market for a star name. George lost no time in making a deal with RKO which brought him aboard under Lesser. Their collaboration resulted in what remains as the best historical documentation of Daniel Boone's life, despite the craze set off by Walt Disney's adaptation two decades later with Fess Parker. Entitled simply *Daniel Boone,* the entire film enjoyed restrained performances by O'Brien, Heather Angel and John Carradine, who was masterful as the villainous Simon Girty.

Tulsa radio singer Ray Whitley was brought in to help George compete with the singing cowboy craze in 1938. An above-average actor for a musical personality, Whitley also supplied some comedy relief. The O'Brien westerns continued to feature top-notch supporting casts which included such soon-to-be-famous ladies as Laraine Day and Rita Hayworth, and the villains he fought were among the best—Fred Kohler, Noah Beery and Slim Whittaker. George's career peaked in 1939 with six westerns and *Triple Justice* temporarily closed out his career; on December 12, 1941, George O'Brien was recalled to active service with the U.S. Navy. During the two decades between wars, he had retained his reserve status and now carried a commission. After a few months working with inductees, he was assigned as a beachmaster, taking part in 15 invasions. Discharged in 1946 as a Commander, George returned to Hollywood for a small role in *My Wild Irish Rose* and supporting roles in *Fort Apache* and *She Wore a Yellow Ribbon* before undertaking a real turkey for Universal called *The Gold Raiders*, co-starring the Three Stooges. It was a rather sad affair for O'Brien fans. Another recall to active duty during the Korean conflict finished his screen career and O'Brien retired from the Navy in 1960.

What had made George O'Brien popular? A simple formula of good pictures and acting ability above that of the average saddle star. Without a doubt he could have enjoyed the same success as a dramatic star, but the athletically inclined actor preferred western adventure to drawing room drama, and for those of us who enjoyed good horse operas in the thirties, he provided some of the most realistic entertainment of the decade. We returned the favor by keeping him on the roster of the top 10 western stars at the box-office from 1932 to 1940, a fair exchange.

David Howard directed several of O'Brien's westerns like **The Rainbow Trail** (1932), with Cecilia Parker.

Greta Nissen and Claire Trevor shared the hero in **Life in the Raw** (1933).

The Cowboy Millionaire, with Edgar Kennedy.

After Sol Lesser cleared the screen rights for **When a Man's a Man,**
Fox produced the picture in 1935 with O'Brien and Dorothy Wilson.

George's westerns featured noted actors like Paul Kelly in support.

They also featured the screen debuts of actresses like Lorraine Johnson. This is a scene from **Arizona Legion** (1939) before she won fame as Laraine Day.

George did his own riding . . .

. . . and stunts in many pictures. These are from **Stage to Chino** (1941

Riders of the Purple Sage (1931).

Jack Randall

OF THE APPARENTLY UNLIMITED NUMBER OF PROGRAM WESTERN STARS
to appear in the thirties, none came closer to having a permanent
flirtation with disaster than one Addison Randall, who happened to
be the brother of another horse opera hero, Bob Livingston. A San
Fernando, California, boy, Randall entered the world of vaudeville
as a singer after completing his college education and first appeared
on the screen playing bit parts in 1934. Three years later, he emerged
at Monogram as the lead in *Riders of the Dawn,* a rather good oater in
spite of several glaring defects.

Although he projected as an interesting hero, Randall's shortcomings initially proved large, but he had made great strides toward over-
coming most of them by 1942 when he left the screen to join the U.S.
Army Air Corps. In those few years, he made but a handful of westerns,
yet Jack Randall created a spot for himself in western cinema lore
not unlike that of Bob Allen and a few others whose trail dust was limited. To begin with, Jack was a virile he-man but he lacked the personal magnetism on screen that produced a big box-office draw. Reviewers caustically referred to him as a "Gary Cooper chassis with a Robert
Taylor face."

Something of a song thrush by trade, his flicks were burdened by
musical numbers complete with instrumental and vocal background
to accompany his solo warbling, causing *Variety* to suggest that perhaps the time had arrived when the light operatic touch of "wagon
wheel harmony and solos badly bayed at the moon" should be per-
manently retired; for those of you who associate the musical western

174

Jack Randall.

with the forties and fifties, remember that this was 1938, only a few years after the cycle had gotten underway. Both Jack's voice and the tunes he offered were unimpressive and his merciless mugging at the camera while he toiled his way through a song brought the small fry to the floor with laughter; a continuation of this nonsense could have completely ruined his career as an action star. But by 1938, Monogram had seen fit to minimize the singing in favor of heroics and Randall's stature began to climb both with critics and patrons.

Unfortunately, Carl Krusada was responsible for many of Jack's scripts and these were done in the same vein in which he had written several serials: one logical question from the viewer (such as Why?) shot the plot from horseback at the opening title. Krusada, who was often accused of writing his scripts on the backs of envelopes while enroute to the studio in the morning, seldom bothered with such mundane questions and unless the audience was willing to accept a good deal on faith, it never fully understood the whys and wherefores of his cinematic epics. For example, in *The Kid from Santa Fe*, Randall took a 50-foot fall over a ravine into the water below, got up and walked away as if he'd just stepped out of bed. But then, Krusada was not alone in sharing responsibility for the credibility gap; someone should have at least made certain that the hero's clothes were wet as he departed from the stream. But in spite of this particular instance, countless others like it, and the fact that alone among the western heroes Jack did not bleed when he was shot, Randall progressed from a rather unsure actor in 1937 to a self-confident (though still dour much of the time) professional when he left the screen.

Much of Jack's reputation revolved around the hard fighting and fast action with which Robert F. Hill filled the short five-reelers that averaged 48 minutes each. Hill was another holdover from the silent era whose abilities as a serial and western director had provided a good living for him over the years and he earned his place in the medium working with hundreds like Jack whose acting ability was minimal. While Randall was occasionally doubled by Yakima Canutt and others, daredevil Jack more often did his own dangerous work, which was filmed in closeups to give the audiences real thrills. It was this very willingness to prove his capabilities that tragically ended Randall's career. Shortly after being discharged from military service in 1945, Jack returned to the movies and signed with Universal to do a serial. During the initial filming of *The Royal Mounted Rides Again*, he took a fatal fall from a horse. His demise at age 39 removed another cowboy from the western scene and proved the fatal blow to a career of ups and downs which many felt was just beginning to show promise.

Buzz Henry and Frank Yaconelli supported Jack in **Trigger Smith** (1939).

Another scene from **Trigger Smith.**

George Chesbro and Bud Osborne plan to keep Jack under wraps in **The Mexicali Kid** (1938).

Who would have believed that Fuzzy Knight was once young? **Where the West Begins** (1938).

With Ernie Adams in **Gun Packer** (1938).

Jack and Dennis Moore in **Wild Horse Canyon** (1939).

Charles King and George Chesbro have the drop on Jack in **Wild Horse Range** (1940).

With Al St. John and Ted Adams in **Gunsmoke Trail** (1938).

If it isn't Charlie King, it's Keene Duncan; somebody always had a gun on our hero. **Covered Wagon Trails** (1940).

Tex Ritter

A GRAND OLD NAME OF COUNTRY AND WESTERN MUSIC (AND THE ONLY member of both the Cowboy Hall of Fame and the Country & Western Music Hall of Fame), Woodward Maurice Ritter earned his spurs during a decade in the movies. One of the few authentic westerners to ride onto the screen during the heyday of the musical B western of the thirties, this graduate of Northwestern's law school had acquired quite a reputation as a traditional folk singer, song writer and radio performer when independent producer Edward Finney signed him for a 1936 screen series to be released by Grand National.

Finney, whose career dated back into the silent era with comedian Johnny Hines, was an imaginative exploiter of the old school, and in Tex Ritter he acquired a genuine property; of all the singing cowboys who were to challenge Gene Autry's fast-growing popularity, Ritter was by far the most talented and interesting, although not the most successful. But recognizing his intrinsic worth as a screen performer, Finney set to work creating yet another celluloid hero and he succeeded to an extent far greater than his modest budgets would have allowed in another's hands.

The Grand National westerns starring Tex Ritter varied in quality, with a few constructed around stock footage which dated back as far as 1915; yet there was a dash and vigor about this new balladeer's personality which set him apart from the competition. While Finney's production and direction talents turned out a fairly good series overall, it was Tex by himself who put them above the average, singing (not acting) his way into the top ten western stars for a period of seven

Tex Ritter.

years. Finney then managed to obtain distribution through Monogram, where Ritter came into his own in the period 1938–41 as a western screen personality. After completing this contract, Tex signed to support Bill Elliott at Columbia in 1941, and the following year he co-starred with Johnny Mack Brown at Universal, where he played some of the most delightful (and best) roles of his career.

The Lone Star Trail found Brown as a paroled convict doing under-cover work in return for his freedom. A condition of this release was the prohibition of guns while completing the assignment and Johnny was forced to use his fists in several roughhouse fight scenes. This created a perfect spot for Tex in the script, who appeared on the scene as a U.S. Marshal assigned to watch over Brown and give him six-gun assistance as the occasion warranted. Ritter brought the role off splendidly in a droll fashion, adding a large plus to an already well-established series.

Joining Dave O'Brien and Guy Wilkinson as one of the "Texas Rangers," Ritter brought his screen career to a close in a 1944 PRC series. While these westerns suffered to a large extent from the same liabilities that afflicted every PRC series (mainly cheap production), the three managed to hold things together reasonably well. Always a bit on the stocky side, Tex had put on a little extra weight over the years, and in the PRC westerns this tended to emphasize his age.

The character which Tex brought to the screen was an unusual combination of the traditional westerner and the singing cowpoke. Although the West in which he rode was not that of Hart or even Mix, it did not lean overly in the direction of 1880 settings with modern dialogue, as was the case with many of the lesser horse opera heroes, whose pictures were virtually interchangeable with B melodramas of the period. All that differed in these was the dress and location, and some B westerns even tried to combine the two, introducing modern gangsters to the old West. For this ring of truth, Ritter had Finney to thank; the producer had attempted as far as possible to keep the Tex Ritter image one of the West, despite the musical interludes, and to Tex's credit he did his best (which was often good) to act within this framework.

As a hero, Tex had a few drawbacks. His Texas drawl was authentic enough, but Tex was a little heavy in size and too youthful looking when he came to the screen. Like Jack Hoxie and others before him, Tex's size and build combined over the years to destroy the leading man image just as his career drew to a close. But Ritter possessed a golden voice, one that was to give him several gold records over a lengthy Capitol recording career, and for many of his fans this was sufficient reason to patronize the neighborhood theatres exhibiting the latest Tex Ritter adventure.

His best work was done at Universal with Brown and as a part

of PRC's *Texas Rangers*. In these two series, Ritter was not required
to carry the entire five reels himself, and so the writers were able to
emphasize his strong points, letting the other leads carry the burden
of dramatic acting. With Brown, this was not difficult and Dave
O'Brien wasn't bad in that department either, although he found far
greater fame as a comedy writer for Red Skelton in later years. If you
can overlook the production flaws, it's not hard to enjoy Tex and his
cohorts in the PRC westerns, yet most of Ritter's pictures had their
own particular charm and no real Tex Ritter fan (and there were
many) will stand for criticism of his hero even today.

Tex kept busy after leaving the screen, and although he was the
composer of many sagebrush ditties, he earned his seat in the country
and western music field with his immensely popular rendition of *High
Noon* for the soundtrack of that picture, and *Hillbilly Heaven,* a recording that draws tears from the misty eyes of those old enough
to identify with its words. Still active at this writing, Tex just completed an unsuccessful bid to enter national politics on the Republican
ticket in Tennessee, but reporters following this 64-year old trouper
on his campaign tour soon discovered that while he might not outdraw
the opposition with ballots, he could still out-sing them any day of
the week.

Starlight over Texas.

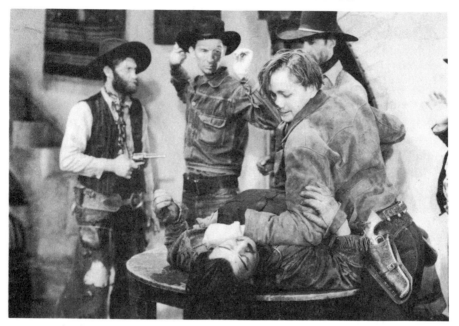

Al St. John kept the fight clean in **Sing Cowboy Sing.**

Ed Finney's productions with Tex were first-rate westerns despite low budgets and stock footage.

Rolling Home to Texas.

Glenn Strange had a few words for Tex in **Rhythm of the Rio Grande.**
Besides popping up in countless westerns, Strange also played the
Frankenstein monster three times and can now be seen on television as
Gunsmoke's bartender.

Tex thinks that this is a friendly game before hitting the trail, but Earl
Dwire and company have a different idea.

Roy Rogers

WITH THE RELEASE OF *Under Western Stars* and its publicity mill grinding out reams of copy about the sensational new star, Republic presented its second singing cowboy to the screen in 1938. While the road to leading roles and western stardom had not been quite so easy for Roy Rogers as Republic wanted audiences to believe, he soon became Gene Autry's chief competition in the musical western arena. As Roy's career closely paralleled that of Autry's in several respects, it has invited the inevitable comparisons between the two made periodically over the years and fans are still divided as to which man was really more popular.

Born Leonard Slye in Cincinnati, Roy had grown up in Portsmouth and Duck Run, Ohio, taking his first job after leaving school in a shoe factory near his home. But he eventually turned up on a New Mexico ranch, where he learned the western skills of roping and riding while occasionally displaying his self-taught musical ability on the guitar by entertaining at neighborhood square dances. Migrating to California in 1930, he played a few radio dates, worked at odd jobs and then changed his name to Dick Weston to team up with Bob Nolan, Tim Spencer and Hugh Farr to form the "Sons of the Pioneers," one of the best of the western musical groups of the period. He also landed small roles in some of Charles Starrett's Columbia westerns, as well as in some of Autry's Republic pictures before being cast in leading roles. But from 1938 on, the path was smooth and Roy Rogers had little difficulty in establishing himself as "The King of the Cowboys."

Roy's screen career started off in low gear; as the ranking cowpoke

The King of the Cowboys.

on the Republic lot, Autry's films received most of the production money and exploitation while Rogers's remained low-budget; but this unequal attention gave Roy an opportunity to develop a style. It also offered him some of the best-written parts he was ever to play—*Billy the Kid Returns, Days of Jesse James, Young Buffalo Bill* and a supporting role in what turned out to be Republic's western epic of 1940, *The Dark Command.* This John Wayne oater detailed the activities of Charles Quantrill and his guerrilla band during the Civil War, with Roy playing Fletcher McCloud, brother of the girl with whom Wayne and Walter Pidgeon (as Quantrill) were in love. His portrayals of western outlaws like Billy the Kid were well done despite extensive character revisions by the writers to present him in a sympathetic light and Roy's sincerity carried them off well.

The low production budgets were primarily responsible for the realism in the early Rogers westerns, but this soon gave way to an increasingly heavy emphasis on the musical format as Republic blatantly attempted to duplicate the successful Autry formula with its new star. Not at all pleased with the build-up given Roy, Gene even left the screen for a time until the difficulties were ironed out to his satisfaction.

Roy's extremely youthful appearance proved to be something of a liability; he never did age sufficiently to impress viewers with his maturity. Somehow, the impression lingered that this cowboy was a perennial 25 and so his script writers were required to take extra caution, inserting dialogue which gave credence to his portrayal of the experienced good guy, usually in the form of a bantering conversation with George "Gabby" Hayes that started off, "Roy, you remember when . . . ?" This established that Roy was indeed an old hand at heroic acts and left audiences wondering how he had survived it all in such good condition.

His slender build also worked against him; the villains were usually much larger and meaner looking than the star, making it difficult to stage convincing fistic duels for the camera and these were avoided when possible for several years. When Roy attempted to look very serious, his eyes tended to close into a semi-squint, giving him the look of one who's not to be completely trusted. While he soon overcame this to some extent, it was difficult for some of us to really accept Roy as a genuine hero, especially in his overblown musical extravaganzas of the mid-forties.

But Rogers was fortunate in other ways; he was a much better actor than most of the other cowboys active at the time, especially those of the musical variety, and once the action began, there was no doubt as to his other abilities, despite the use of occasional doubles. Roy also possessed a good voice and was backed up by the Sons of the Pioneers and later Foy Willing and his Riders of the Purple Sage. Unlike the musical groups that supported Gene Autry, those working with Roy were generally cast as ranch hands and were responsible for an integral and sometimes pivotal action in the story. This technique of working them into the script instead of simply tacking them on for the musical numbers made it a little easier for youngsters to sit through such periodic breaks in the action.

Roy had two first-rate foils in Gabby Hayes and later Pat Brady. Gabby could even act on occasion and became an institution on the program western screen; Pinky Lee proved a distraction and didn't last, nor did Andy Devine. Roy's horse Trigger was billed as "The Smartest Horse in the Movies" and this 1100-pound golden palomino could perform 52 separate and distinct tricks, making him a star in his own right and convincing fans that no matter how badly things went for the hero, the horse could always save the day if need be.

Roy's early westerns often featured Mary Hart as the feminine interest and the two were billed as "The Sweethearts of the West"; but it was with Dale Evans, who rose from supporting roles to co-star status, that Rogers really hit his stride. A Texas girl who had worked for a Memphis insurance company while trying to break into radio, Dale was brought to Hollywood with Anson Weeks's orchestra by Paramount, but her career leveled off at that point. With her ambition to become a dramatic actress frustrated, Dale took the western parts offered her by Republic and suddenly found fan mail pouring in. Anxious to capitalize on her popularity, the studio increased her roles and watched the letters double. Rogers and Evans worked well with each other in spite of Dale's initial dislike for sagebrush roles, and two years after his wife Arlene passed away, The King of the Cowboys married the Queen of the West in a New Year's Eve ceremony in 1947.

As the musical western cycle ran its course in the late forties, production budgets zoomed and suddenly Rogers's westerns began to emphasize action, with Roy emerging in Trucolor as a champion of justice whose fists spoke louder than his six-guns. The man-to-man encounters avoided early in his career now played a prominent role and the gun became a last resort. While many youngsters were unable to understand why most of their heroes had holstered the trusty six-shooter (which inevitably fired dozens of times without apparent re-loading), they were unaware that the B western was about to bite the dust. Television, declining audiences and rising costs were the villains and Roy finally left the theatrical screen in 1951.

Rogers entered the business world as had Gene Autry. An NBC tv series produced by and featuring Roy ran 5½ years before going into syndication. Appearing on radio, tv, with circuses and rodeos, Roy kept busy and his name and endorsement graced a collection of 360 items from binoculars to books, grossing over $34 million in 1954. Roy and Dale became noted for their charitable works, many of which benefited children, and survived several personal tragedies. Today the duo occasionally make tv appearances together and in millions of homes across the country, viewers change channels, sitting back in their easy chairs to briefly recapture a youthful memory as one of their seemingly indestructible heroes breaks into song once more and carries them back 30 years to a Saturday matinee.

Alden Chase and Carol Hughes look on as Roy hams it up in **Under Western Stars,** his first starring role.

Roy Rogers in an early starring role.

With both guns leveled at Harry Wood's back, Roy holds the entire gang at bay in **Come on Rangers** (1938).

Rough Riders Roundup (1939).

The Arizona Kid (1939) with Fred Burns and Gabby Hayes. Gabby's apparent age contrasted greatly with Roy's youth, giving almost a father-son relationship on-screen.

Roy as Fletcher McCloud in **The Dark Command** (1940).

With Bob Steele and Noah Beery Jr. in **Canyon City Kid** (1940).

Jim Corey had better beware; when Roy squinted that much he was plain mad. A veteran villain from Hoot Gibson's era, Corey had much experience menacing heroes. From **Robin Hood of the Pecos** (1941).

Mary Lee had a brief run of popularity as a Republic heroine. From
Song of Nevada (1944) with Roy and Lloyd Corrigan.

Down Dakota Way (1949) with Monte Montana and Dale Evans.

Roy and Dale Evans in **Utah** (1945), before she became "The Queen of the West." The background is a painted backdrop.

Reb Russell

WHILE MOST RAGS-TO-RICHES STORIES ARE TAKEN FOR GRANTED BY THOSE who hear of them, the fact that hard work, determination and disappointments are an integral part of any Alger story is often overlooked. We've already mentioned several football heroes who swapped their pigskins for saddle fame in the early thirties, but there's one more who can't be neglected—Fay H. Russell, better known to western fans as Reb.

He was born in Paola, Kansas, in 1905, but the family moved to Coffeyville after his father's death two years later and as soon as he was old enough, the boy went to work to help his mother support the family. To this point, his story is not unlike that of many of his generation (including my own father), but with Reb, a man named Walter Johnson provided the edge that the boy needed to rise above adversity. The pitching ace of the Washington Senators at the time, Johnson made Coffeyville his home in the off-season and often worked out with Reb and other neighborhood youngsters, all of whom idolized "The Big Train." One of Reb's earliest memories is that of the welcoming parade held for Johnson. Everyone of importance was there; bands played and men spoke highly of his accomplishments. Reb decided that it would be just like that for him one day and this decision played a major role in what was to come.

With such an incentive, young Russell progressed through a variety of forgotten schools, but gained a reputation in athletics as he went, and as a freshman at Nebraska in 1927 he began to emerge in the national spotlight. A sophomore in 1928, he was selected as the All-

Reb Russell.

Star quarterback of the Big Six (now Eight) team and his hard-driving field activities earned him a spot in Ripley's "Believe It or Not" column. After transferring to Northwestern in 1930, he played fullback, where against Notre Dame Russell by himself gained only four yards less than the entire Notre Dame squad. Three times he led the Wildcats the length of the field and while his team lost 14–0 to the Irish, Knute Rockne tabbed Russell as the greatest line plunger of all time. That same year, he joined the ranks of football's immortals when he was named All-American fullback.

Reb played in only one game in 1931, and this resulted in a scene exactly like those used by hack writers for collegiate gridiron dramas. The All-American fullback sat on the bench with three misplaced vertebrae in his back and the Wildcats were trailing 6–0 in the final quarter. Begging the coach to let him play, Reb went in carrying an 11-pound brace on his back. He drove to the goal, leading the team to a 7–6 decision. Enter Universal Pictures with a contract for a role in Richard Arlen's *The All-American* (1932) and Reb Russell temporarily abandoned the football field for a sound stage.

Pro football beckoned in 1932 with an offer to join the New York Giants; in 1933, he was traded to the Philadelphia Eagles for whom he played his greatest game, and the one Reb considers to be his pro career in a capsule. Almost by himself, Russell stopped Red Grange and Bronco Nagurski, holding the Chicago Bears to a 3–3 tie. Now along came Sol Lesser, who placed the star athlete under a two-year contract and gave him the lead in *When a Man's a Man*, which was to start filming on location in Utah. But author Harold Bell Wright stepped in, claiming that he had sold only the silent screen rights and a lawsuit followed. All Hollywood awaited the outcome of this trial, for if the studios were forced to repurchase talkie rights to stories they owned, it could have proven disastrous in the midst of the Depression.

Reb drew his salary during the two-year fight and waited, but when Lesser finally won, the producer had lost interest in both his star and the story. In the meantime, Tom Mix had taken a liking to Reb, who accompanied the famous cowboy to many Hollywood parties and social gatherings, where Tom introduced him to producers and directors. Through Mix's efforts, Reb signed with Willis Kent in 1935 for 12 westerns, the total of his screen career. With Bart Carre as production manager and many veteran actors in supporting roles, Reb delivered some surprisingly good pictures for independent productions. His first featured Gabby Hayes in support; Gabby taught Reb how to use makeup properly and gave him many tips on acting. According to Reb, who looks back on his film career with detachment, you only needed two expressions to be a western actor—constipation and relief.

Among the top talents with whom Reb worked was a slender young stuntman, Yakima Canutt. While Yak did most of the falls from the horses, he taught Russell some of the finer points of stunting, and between the two they devised some interesting effects. In *Man from Hell*, Reb was about to be hanged as a horse thief. Yak constructed a system of piano wires tied to Reb's back and when the noose tightened, Reb was "strung up" via the unseen wires, but censors thought the scene too realistic and it was removed from the release print.

When Reb completed his contract, no other offers were forthcoming and so he went to Chicago to negotiate a daily radio show like that of Tom Mix for Quaker Oats. The pilot was produced but the series died on the vine. Meeting Phil Isley while on a personal appearance tour, Reb was talked into touring with a circus act. Tom Mix, who was on tour at the time, advised Reb to do it and with the help of Pawnee Bill Lillie, Reb assembled a show featuring himself and other top acts. Reb did trick riding, rope spinning and whip tricks, touring until 1940 when he retired to a large ranch near Kansas City.

During his years running the Blue River Ranch, he devised a scheme of diversified ranching-farming without government subsidy, and in 1951 he returned to Kansas and a 2500-acre ranch. Carrying his ideas to the people, Reb ran unsuccessfully for Congress in 1965. Although his career encompassed three areas of show business, Reb never ceases to be amazed at just how many former admirers he still has, and like Al Hoxie in the silent era, enjoys a position in western screen nostalgia out of proportion to his 12 starring roles; but Reb still weighs in at his college weight of 220 and works each day on the ranch, welcoming fans from across the country with a warm, friendly handshake and smile.

Outlaw Rule.

With Yakima Canutt in **Fighting Thru.**

Blazing Guns with Joseph Girard.

Fighting Thru.

Reb and Bob Kortman in **Blazing Guns.**

Fred Scott

ALTHOUGH KEN MAYNARD AND OTHER WESTERN STARS HAD WARBLED A
tune or two on-screen almost before talkie technology was perfected,
the musical western vogue that diluted the genre to one of near-
ludicrous proportions did not arrive on the scene until Gene Autry
made his debut as a Son of the West in 1934. But once producers
caught on, singing cowboy stars came into their own right, and for
a few years few self-respecting screen cowpokes in the program western could hold their heads up high unless they had a voice, either their
own or one dubbed for them. One of this lengthy parade that rode
across the celluloid range in the thirties and forties was Fred Scott,
whose screen career dated back to 1920 and small roles in innumerable
slapstick comedies.

Leaving pictures shortly after sound arrived to seek his fortune
elsewhere, Scott spent several years singing with the San Francisco
Opera but the lure of the screen was too great; after doing a near-
perfect parody of the singing cowboy in RKO's *The Last Outlaw*
(1936), a chance meeting with Jed Buell brought him back to the
screen as a cowboy hero in his own starring series. Buell, a former
public relations man for the Mack Sennett studio who was acquainted
with Fred's voice, was set to produce a series of horse operas in co-
operation with George H. Callaghan for Spectrum Pictures and Scott
became his star.

Although these Scott westerns for Spectrum were independent productions made on the proverbial shoestring, they proved to be fast-
action epics and received fairly good notices. Typical of the lot, *The*

Fred Scott.

Roaming Cowboy opened and closed with a gunfight, moving so
rapidly there was hardly sufficient time for the hero to catch his breath
long enough to belt out a tune, but he did. With directors like
Sam Newfield and Robert F. Hill calling the shots, Scott appeared
to be a sure bet to move on to better things. He was tall, good looking
in a he-man way and a pretty fair singer. He had the benefit of feminine leads like Lois January, who could act and ride in addition to
looking pretty for the cameras. As looking pretty seemed to be the
major requirement in casting most young actresses as western heroines
at the time, Miss January was a welcome relief. Al St. John furnished
the comedy relief and even Stan Laurel dropped by to furnish ideas
for humorous sequences and money for production. By all rights, the
Scott image should have emerged full-blown except for one thing—
Fred was not exactly an actor, at least where dialogue was concerned,

and while others with the same handicap became top box-office attractions, Scott had no Republic or Universal studio working in his behalf.

Lesser measures to boost his popularity and acquaint the country with Fred Scott (such as personal appearance tours) were tried before beginning another Spectrum series, but by the completion of the fourth in the group, the company was out of business and the lad who had everything going in his direction suddenly found that he was a surplus commodity—the range was overcrowded with singing troubadours. Leaving motion pictures in 1942 after completing *Rodeo Rhythm*, Fred popped up in the Florentine Gardens Review as singer-manager and then in M-G-M's sound department before entering Los Angeles real estate, where he became a well-known figure.

Although he was offered other screen roles over the years, Fred and Hollywood had parted for good. He left his admirers with only a few memories. But while he made only a handful of starring westerns, Fred Scott's name still comes up whenever sagebrush fans get together, recalling the likes of Reb Russell and Tex Fletcher.

Fred's cheerful smile and golden vocal cords went hand-in-hand with a brace of six-shooters.

The Roaming Cowboy, with Al St. John.

Fred and Jack Merton have a surprise ahead of them beyond that door.

Harry Harvey has a bone to pick with Jack Merton, but Fred has a blonde on his mind. **The Two Gun Troubador.**

Fred's disguise in **The Fighting Deputy** reminded western fans of William Desmond's Riddle Rider of the silent era. Note the dime-store Hallowe'en mask.

Randolph Scott

AS A YOUNG BOY GROWING UP IN A SMALL VERMONT TOWN, I WAS FORtunate enough to live next door to the most fascinating edifice in the entire county; one that allowed my imagination to escape the rural boundaries of Northern New England. Inside the Park Theatre's 30-foot lobby, one wall was decorated with a long frame in which the manager placed a lobby card announcing each coming attraction well in advance of its scheduled screening date. When one film had played its run, the corresponding card was withdrawn, all were moved forward and another placed at the end, giving patrons an enticing glimpse of the delights in store for future weeks. For us youngsters, the westerns and serials held the most interest, and while Charles Starrett, Johnny Mack Brown, Buck Jones and others promised exciting moments to come, one particular western star caught my fancy as did no others in a lengthy career of moviegoing.

He didn't restrict himself to westerns alone until around 1947, nor did he appear in the same inexpensive black and white oaters as our other heroes; that may have been part of the reason that I enjoyed Randolph Scott so much. His horse operas were different and the appearance of a lobby card announcing the imminent arrival of his latest adventure signalled a countdown filled with anticipation that grew as the appointed date neared. For me, Randolph Scott had a strong appeal all his own and only Bill Elliott ever began to approach the adulation I held as a youngster for this gentleman of the West.

A native of Orange County, Virginia, Scott had attended Georgia Tech and the University of North Carolina, touring Europe and work-

Randolph Scott.

ing in the family business before arriving in Los Angeles for what he termed a lengthy rest. A golf date with Howard Hughes resulted in an interview with Cecil B. deMille, and at the director's suggestion Scott joined the Pasadena Community Playhouse, coming to the screen two years later with a role in Paramount's *Sky Bride* (1931). His appearances grew in size and important over the next few years while the erudite Southerner began to develop a distinctive style. Reviewers of the mid-thirties were fond of comparing Randy to Gary Cooper, commenting upon their similarities, which did little to help the soft-spoken Scott's career. Yet he continued to receive choice assignments, playing numerous and varied parts including several western roles and that of Hawkeye in *The Last of the Mohicans*.

Scott's early westerns like *The Man of the Forest* and *Heritage of the Desert* were reasonably solid screen translations of the Zane Grey stories and could hardly be considered B pictures, but at that point in his career, Randy was really too distinguished and handsome. His appeal became much greater as he grew older, with lines and wrinkles beginning to crisscross his weathered face. There was a strong element of identification as the soft-spoken voice emanating from the screen became first that of an older brother and then a father image, and as Randy and I aged together year after year in the darkened theatres across the country, I felt that I had known him all my life.

Unlike most of the other sagebrush stars, Scott's voice and manners were quite distinctive; culture and good breeding fairly oozed from his every pore and a sense of quiet dignity lent an air of strength and authority possessed by few others who rode the range. Whether it was running the Overland Stage in *Westbound*, or laying track for *Canadian Pacific*, Scott left no doubt that he was more than equal to the task and no Indian tribe or band of scheming outlaws could delay the inevitable for long.

Scott's approach in his later westerns bore a marked resemblance to the style of William S. Hart; his simple dress and carefully chosen locations brought a feeling of austere reality to his films augmented by Scott's choice of roles. Like Hart, Randy played both lawman and outlaw with equal conviction and it mattered little which side of the law he was on when the picture opened—you knew he was a hero. Playing the pursuer in roles like *The Bounty Hunter*, a sense of dogged determination filled the screen, yet many of these roles were among the least believable Scott vehicles. While it seemed logical that this man might be involved in a single-minded manhunt for the scoundrels who had killed his wife, mother or best friend years before, somehow it was altogether improbable that Scott could make his living hunting others for profit.

But it was not at all difficult to fit him in as Wyatt Earp (*Frontier Marshal*) or Bat Masterson (*Trail Street*) and just as easy to find him with a price on his head. When scripting history for his portrayals in outlaw epics like *The Doolins of Oklahoma* and *Gunfighter*, certain liberties were invariably taken with the characterization in a calculated attempt at gaining audience sympathy. Yet the self-assurance that Scott projected was sufficient for audiences to accept him as one who could and did tread on and over that fine line between good and evil, and it was not discomforting to find him fast friends with a wanted man, an exercise in acting which few of the other screen westerners could carry off without a discordant note. The sense of reality was strong in Randy's westerns—he seldom played the undercover agent who joined the gang to learn its leader's identity or the numerous other artificial roles which harried script writers were forced to pen for heroes who appeared on the screen in a new adventure every 60 days. Perhaps Scott's greatest appeal can be found in the word *actor;* unlike Sunset Carson, Monte Hale and many others, Randolph Scott was an accomplished actor, and while his western portrayals included some of the elements found in their exploits, he brought a dimension to his roles they were unable to muster.

Scott delivered best as the loner whose past kept popping up as he rode along. He needed and used no comic sidekick; the appearance of crusty Edgar Buchanan in many of the Scott westerns served a similar and much more useful role. Romance was a byproduct of the adventure and by the time Scott had limited his talents to westerns, his age showed sufficiently for romance to be accepted as something that had passed from his grasp. The few roles in which he tried to carry on an affair with the opposite sex were among his weakest, yet Randy's pictures always featured the best-looking fillies available to Central Casting.

But this was not unusual. His westerns were expensive in comparison to those of Republic, Columbia, Universal and RKO, and abounded in production values. Clever but dedicated villains along the order of Victory Jory, David Brien and Zachary Scott plotted his downfall and some darn near accomplished their ends. Scott had the good fortune to be associated with Harry Joe Brown, who had masterminded Ken Maynard's rise to fame in the twenties; the later Scott westerns were co-productions by the two men, and as the B western disappeared in the early fifties, Randy's two pictures yearly were even more valued by western fans.

After *Ride the High Country*, Scott retired, ending a career of almost 30 years on the screen. This last picture was particularly admired by critics who had so often taken the star to task for a lack of forcefulness in his acting, yet this very quality had contributed greatly to Scott's image of the westerner. Like Hart before him, Randolph Scott projected (at least for his fans) an inner conviction and strength that belied his seeming reluctance to do battle unless it was absolutely necessary. We knew Randy would inevitably triumph because he had what it took to win; others won because their writers had preordained it.

Heritage of the Desert (1933) featured this brawling scene with Guinn "Big Boy" Williams.

With Verna Hillie in **Man of the Forest** (1933).

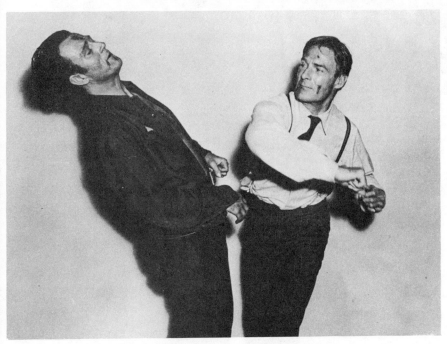

The Spoilers (1942) with John Wayne.

Guinn Williams, Glenn Ford and Randy in **The Desperadoes** (1943).

As Scott lost his youthful looks, his western portrayals took on an added dimension.

Sheriff Charles Kemper has choice words for Randy in **The Gunfighter** (1947).

Barbara Britton and Dorothy Hart both had eyes for Scott in **The Gunfighter.** Miss Hart was true-blue, but Miss Britton portrayed an impetuous younger sister whose betrayal almost cost Randy his life.

The Doolins of Oklahoma (1949).

Zachary Scott gave another of his superb mad-bandit portrayals in **Colt .45** (1950).

The Cariboo Trail (1950).

With Warner Anderson in **Santa Fe** (1951).

Randy's not taking any nonsense from the boys in **Man Behind the Gun** (1952).

With Joan Weldon in **Riding Shotgun** (1954). Scott's westerns were realistic and rugged and Randy never let the fans down.

Charles Starrett

FEW WESTERN STARS RODE FASTER, FOUGHT HARDER, SAVED MORE INNO-
cent lives or sent more outlaws to their just rewards than a steel-eyed
Dartmouth graduate whose grim visage peered over a black kerchief
mask and who answered to the name Durango Kid. Another of the
handsome dramatic actors whose screen career began during that
turbulent period when Hollywood was learning to talk, Charles Starrett's fascination with the motion picture began in 1926 while still an
undergraduate. A member of the Dartmouth football team, the muscular Athol, Massachusetts lad worked as an extra in Richard Dix's
The Quarterback, and once his degree work was completed, he enrolled in New York's American Academy of Dramatic Art before joining the Stewart Walker Stock Company. Starrett came to the screen
in *Damaged Love,* a 1929 Sono Art release, and then began an association with Paramount that proved financially rewarding during the
Depression years; but while entertaining and even delightful, roles
in films like *The Sweetheart of Sigma Chi, So Red the Rose* and *Mur-
der on the Campus* did little to advance his career beyond that of
minor pictures.

The renaissance of the western in the early thirties created a surprising number of cowboy stars; it almost seemed as if a producer
lurked behind every potted plant in Hollywood just waiting to sign
and star would-be talent, and in 1936 Starrett tossed over his dramatic
career to sign with Columbia in return for his own starring series.
He was to last 17 consecutive seasons as a sagebrush hero, winning
his own unique place in the program western's Hall of Fame and his

The Cowboy Star (1936) was one of the best of Charles Starrett's early westerns.

fans' memories. Columbia westerns were never far above the assembly-line level and technically they paled in comparison to the thrill-packed adventures produced at Republic, whose inheritance of Nat Levine's Mascot Pictures with its tradition of fast-moving action influenced its product for almost two decades. But in Starrett, Columbia had a western star worth exploiting, and for several years, it did just that in well-worn plots used time and again. Tall, lean and athletic, his facial features were sharply defined and the jutting jaw of his profile accentuated the look of grim determination that became his trademark. Without a smile, he was the personification of the strong silent man of the West, and except during the inevitable and interminable musical or romantic interludes, Charlie seldom smiled. Coming to the western screen just as its musical vogue began, Starrett was unable to avoid this influence despite his inability to sing, but like Tim Holt, his pictures featured the unpleasantry of small-time groups like the Georgia Crackers, providing an opportunity for sidekick Smiley Burnette to demonstrate why he had been nicknamed "Frog" and cutting down on the production costs involved in telling the story.

For the most part, the Starrett westerns of the thirties were unusually good for Columbia productions, presenting the star as a two-fisted man of action; but as the forties arrived the formula picture was carried to its logical absurdity—each Starrett western featured practically the same cast and the plot twists were too few and far between to tell the stories apart. As a result, this mass production approach made it virtually impossible to differentiate one from another. As an actor, Starrett was up to his task, although the monotony involved in grinding out six to eight films yearly eventually took its toll on the star. Dialogue gradually was minimized in favor of action and the heroic figure he portrayed acquired a serious, quiet demeanor by default.

This style of non-acting stood Starrett in good stead with the beginning of his Durango Kid westerns in the forties; a shadowy Robin Hood of the West dressed entirely in black and riding a black stallion as he battled injustice while wanted by the law was a fascinating premise but at Columbia it soon fell into the same old rut. And yet, Starrett is best remembered today for these roles. Invariably cast as Steve Ramsey or Ransom, Starrett assumed a dual personality as the Durango Kid, the mere mention of whose name would strike terror in the hearts of villains. To those of us in the matinee audience, the five reels of a Durango Kid western equalled a fine Saturday afternoon's entertainment, and we never questioned the gaping inconsistencies which appeared in each and every one. As none of the Durango Kid westerns have played tv to my knowledge, here's a brief outline of the plot of all: the existence of a rancher (or town) was threatened by an outlaw (or gang) when a tall stranger rode into the picture looking for work. Immediately after his arrival, the rustlers (or stagecoach robbers) were thwarted by a masked man in black whose six-shooters spoke with deadly accuracy, yet rarely did the outlaw leader make the obvious connection between the two events. As the Durango Kid was usually sought by the authorities (an honest error on their part) for a crime he had not committed, he could confide in no one and the local lawman was as much a threat as were the outlaws. Not even his sidekick was in on the deception, and operating in this limbo the Kid carried a sort of built-in audience sympathy, especially since we knew that when the nefarious scheme was inadvertently revealed in Starrett's presence, the real hero also knew.

But the inconsistencies we never noted at such an innocent age included such absurdities as Starrett disappearing behind a clump of bushes or even a tree, reappearing almost at once as the masked rider, complete with a black horse. It was easy enough to tell ourselves that his black horse was planted there with the clothes in a saddle bag, but looking back from the vantage point of years, one wonders now just how he happened to have everything on the north range where it would be needed instead of one of the other three points of the compass. And what happened to the other horse? Who knows?

Barry Shipman wrote many of the Durango Kid scripts, and with Fred Sears and Ray Nazarro directing, the emphasis was placed on action instead of logic, harkening back two decades to *The Riddle Rider* and William Desmond's black moustache disguise—none of us ever figured how the villains, who usually had the Durango Kid in their clutches at least once during the picture, could escape identifying the voice or even resist the temptation to pull down the black kerchief for a brief peek at their captive's real identity; yet neither catastrophe ever occurred, and as the last reel faded from the screen, only Charlie and the audience knew the entire truth.

In spite of such mind-bending inanities, the Durango Kid westerns proved popular and remained as one of the better Columbia series until rising production economics almost totally destroyed the character's credibility. By 1949, cost had accelerated into the $60,000+ bracket and remained at that figure only by careful trimming of all possible corners. The Durango Kid's appearances became three- and four-day shooting affairs, as stock footage and entire sequences from his earlier westerns were lifted and written into the shortened scripts. Starrett's age began to show rather noticeably even though he had retained the slim trim figure of a decade before and Jock O'Mahoney frequently doubled the star in the Durango Kid's action scenes. The black face mask made such deception easy and none of us ever doubted for a moment that it was really our hero behind the disguise. Nor were we aware that the days of our favorite cinema fare were limited; even the sloppy editing, lack of a plausible opening and the puzzling ending suddenly thrown at us in such "epics" as *Across the Badlands* (1950) were attributed by those of us "in the know" to our less fortunate companions as the result of a "badly worn print."

After more than 500 reels in the saddle, Charles Starrett retired in 1953, and the Durango Kid disappeared from the screen with him. Looking at the prints in collectors' hands today, it seems quite impossible that we were fascinated by such pedestrian nonsense, yet it was all harmless fun and escapism at its best. Despite its increasingly absurd programming, television has been unable to re-create the same atmosphere that prevailed in a darkened theatre on Saturday afternoon and living rooms or dens lack the excitement of a horde of youngsters thrilling to the chase—perhaps the Durango Kid is needed once again; he'd get quite a hearty welcome from millions who remember.

Spoilers of the Range (1939).

With Hank Newman, Smiley Burnette and Helen Mowing in **The Fighting Frontiersman** (1946).

Starrett lands a haymaker in **Riding Through Nevada** (1942). He put as much gusto into his fight scenes as any program western star.

Jack Mahoney doubled Starrett in **The Durango Kid**'s action scenes . . .

. . . but our hero stood in for the closeups. From **Challenge of the Range** (1949).

With Marjorie Stapp in **The Blazing Trail** (1949).

Starrett could be almost as mean as Bill Elliott. **The Blazing Trail.**

Across the Badlands (1950).

Jimmy Wakely

UPON REACHING THIS POINT IN OUR STORY, YOU MAY RIGHTLY HAVE concluded that stardom in the program westerns of the sound era came to those with one of two greatly divergent backgrounds; exgridiron heroes from Dartmouth and country-western warblers from the heart of Dixie. As a broad generalization this held true, with the football quarterbacks affecting the strong, silent posture and the guitar-strumming troubadours offering competition in the guise of singing cowboys. Jimmy Wakely was one of the latter, and in some ways one of the best of his kind.

Wakely was an Arkansas boy who grew up in Oklahoma and exercised an early predilection for country music by teaming up with Johnny Bond and Scotty Harrel around 1937 to form a trio which gained a certain amount of notoriety and even popularity while picking and singing on Oklahoma City radio stations. This exposure led to an engagement with the famed National Barn Dance which was beamed nation-wide from Tulsa, a recording contract with Decca Records and even occasional appearances on Gene Autry's Melody Ranch broadcasts. By 1939, the Jimmy Wakely Trio had the world of country music firmly in the palm of its hand when along came a Hollywood talent scout with an offer Wakely couldn't resist.

Later that same year, Jimmy made his screen debut in Roy Rogers's *Saga of Death Valley* for Republic. This was followed by appearances in a few of the Autry westerns before Jimmy landed a contract at Universal, where his trio provided the presupposed musical interludes in the Johnny Mack Brown westerns. With Tex Ritter on board to

Jimmy Wakely and Lee "Lasses" White in **Song of the Range** (1944).

support Brown, the musical content of Johnny's oaters became just a bit overbearing; but a year later, Jimmy and his group (now called the Saddle Pals) moved over to Columbia where they performed the same rites for another of the strong, silent heroes, Charles Starrett. In 1944, Wakely made the giant leap from musical supporting roles to leads with a contract at Monogram, and for the next five years, he rode the range in a lengthy series of westerns that varied greatly in quality.

Teamed with Lee "Lasses" White at the outset, Wakely's early Monogram films were small-scale copies of Gene Autry's successful vehicles; Jimmy's producers attempted to duplicate the imitation right down to the ostentatious dress of their newest screen find. As a hero in his own right, the soft-spoken Wakely left a good deal to be desired; a capable enough singer (who even wrote a good share of the less-than-memorable ballads that cluttered the sound track) in his own right, he was hardly the virile he-man on screen and small fry in the audience often found it difficult to distinguish him from their own teen-age brothers.

Lacking both sufficient force and polish in his delivery to give a convincing performance as a rough-and-ready hero, Jimmy's salvation came with his songs. With a pre-established following from his radio days (many of whom supported his recording activities faithfully), he possessed a small but loyal following whose attendance with their youngsters kept the Wakely series solvent; but times were changing, and in an attempt to move with them, several alterations were made in the format of his pictures around 1947.

Walter Taylor, known variously as "Dub" and "Cannonball," replaced White as sidekick and comic relief; musical groups such as Wesley Tuttle's Texas Stars, Woody Woodel's Riding Rangers, The Guadalajara Trio and Wakely's own Saddle Pals found their services no longer required, and dispensing with the colorful costumes in favor of more workmanlike garb, our hero assumed a posture more or less in accord with the non-singing horse opera heroes, while continuing to belt a ballad or two per picture. This effort to establish Jimmy as a hard-riding, two-fisted Son of the Golden West produced little but consternation at the box office. Loyal followers of the silver vocal cords were disappointed and youngsters who reveled in the fantasy of blazing six-guns and barroom brawls were less than impressed.

The long ride came to an end in 1949 when Wakely read the handwriting on the wall. Work in a few feature efforts for other studios followed before one last series was made at Columbia, but by this time the meager following of Jimmy Wakely fans had dissipated almost completely. One of the most outstanding features of sagebrush stardom was that those who did not appear on the screen with regularity soon found themselves searching for their former audiences, most of whom seemed to have scattered to the four winds. Producing a few of his own features in the early fifties, Wakely dropped into supporting roles (still carrying his guitar) before leaving the screen to manage his music company and recording work.

Still active today as a country and western singer, Jimmy's outstanding attribute as a western star rested in his voice; but coming along when the screen was virtually glutted with crooning cowpokes, he was unable to hold his own in the action arena, which really made or broke a star in the eyes of the audience (mainly kids) and passed from the scene just as the program western began to die. Interesting speculation for an evening by the fireplace could easily revolve around what might have happened to Wakely had Autry's producers latched onto him first.

Moon over Montana (1945).

"Rough 'em up, Jimmy boy!" **Trail to Mexico** (1946).

A rousing moment from **Song of the Sierras** (1946). Such scenes pleased his vocal fans but the kids shrunk into their seats in horror as another song burst forth.

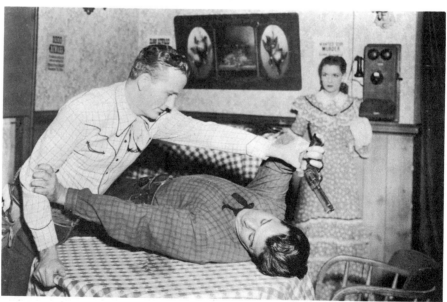

See, Jimmy could fight as well as sing. **Oklahoma Blues** (1947).

Silver Trails (1948).

With Walter "Cannonball" Taylor in **Brand of Fear** (1949).

"Looks like we've got the answer." **Roaring Westward** (1949).

Jimmy's screen career closed out with small roles like that of the singing trooper in **Arrow in the Dust** (1954).

Whip Wilson

NOVELTIES ON THE SCREEN ALWAYS SEEM TO GUARANTEE SOME DEGREE of success, at least for a time, and the western actor who could use something like a bullwhip with expertise in place of a gun or his fists was certainly different. Of the three western leading men who performed with a whip on the sagebrush screen, Charles Meyers was without a doubt the most accomplished at his trade. Although born in Texas in 1919, Meyers was brought up and educated in Illinois where he worked at a variety of odd jobs after completing his schooling. But odd jobs gave way to a form of wanderlust and he returned to Texas to learn the ins and outs of the rodeo business. Meyers became quite adept at the various arts required by a rodeo personality and was doing nicely in this form of show business when World War II broke out. Giving it up to join the U.S. Marines, he saw action in most of the major battles of the South Pacific before being discharged.

Resuming his career on the rodeo circuit, Meyers was spotted by a movie talent scout and made his screen debut in one of Jimmy Wakely's 1948 Monogram oaters, *Silver Trails*. He delivered the goods sufficiently well to sign immediately with the company for his own starring series, acquiring a new name (Whip Wilson) and a sidekick along the way—veteran comic Andy Clyde rode with him until his brief career came to a close a few years later.

Somewhat on the stocky side with a round cherubic face, Whip Wilson made a rather indifferent hero in spite of the production effort which was put into his initial pictures, and as the B western slid down-

241

Whip Wilson.

hill to its finish, so did the quality of Whip's films. Had he arrived on the screen a decade before Wilson might have become a popular leading man, despite his obvious shortcomings as an actor, or so the story goes. He certainly filled the bill as far as the action sequences went, but how long could any non-actor count on a snapping bullwhip to carry him along? While the brief careers of many western actors have been attributed to arriving on the screen at a point too late in time, this is really a most questionable explanation, and certainly so in the case of Whip Wilson. But the novelty of his prowess with the whip was almost sufficient to keep him going in spite of his poor acting and he definitely made good use of the skill. While Sunset Carson had occasionally settled an altercation with the slender instrument, he had virtually passed from the scene as an important western star when Wilson arrived and the only competition Whip faced came from one Lash LaRue, who ranked a rather poor second in what he could do with the thonged leather.

But the proof of the pudding comes in how believable the man appears to his audience, and while the chunky rodeo rider gave it his best, the youngsters seemed to catch a lack of reality about Wilson's adventures between the snarling flashes of his whip. His scripts were constructed to take every possible advantage of the gimmick and Whip even rode his way through plate glass windows on it, reminiscent of a tumbleweed Tarzan. There seemed to be little he couldn't and didn't do with it, and while variety demanded that Whip occasionally unlimber the shooting iron, his reliance on that traditional western weapon for meting out justice was slight. Caught by a snapping whip, villains came sailing off fast-moving horses or over saloon hitching posts with a regularity that defied logic; one wonders why they never thought of standing back far enough to gun him down in good old western fashion. In fact, some of the stunts that Whip pulled off with the leather thong, while realistic enough, were just far-fetched enough to bring whoops of amazement from the kids, who didn't believe their eyes—after you had seen a couple of his oaters, you'd seen them all.

When Monogram-Allied Artists halted its B western production, Wilson retired from the screen, although the cracking whip continued to stand him in good stead with appearances at rodeos, circuses and even on television until his untimely death at age 45 in 1964. While Whip Wilson may not have ranked with the best, he certainly was different, and if you live a good clean life, you may even catch his old movies on television and learn what the critter was all about.

Riders of the Dusk (1949).

Whip Wilson in a scene from **Silver Raiders** (1950).

Now really, is that any way to enter a saloon? **Haunted Trails** (1948).

Gunslingers (1950).

With Fuzzy Knight, Jim Bannon and Lane Bradford in **The Stagecoach Driver** (1951).

While he relied heavily on the whip, Wilson could slug it out . . .

. . . or even shoot it out. From **Arizona Territory** (1950) with Andy Clyde and Nancy Saunders.

This is what the West was all about? **Nevada Badmen** (1951).

And Others

THE SILENT PROGRAM WESTERN EXISTED FOR 26 YEARS; ITS TALKIE COUN-
terpart lasted only 24 years before succumbing to a variety of factors
that it was no longer virile enough to overcome. In a sense, the program westerns was bushwhacked, done in by a sneaky punch from
behind by an economic undercutting of the ground on which it had
once so proudly stood. Like many other fond memories of years past,
the B western can never return in its pure theatrical form; the audience
is fast diminishing and what appears today on the small tv tube is
hardly a substitute for the sweep and grandeur once afforded by the
large screen.

As an art and entertainment form, the western will probably never
really die, but as with all other forms of cinematic endeavor, it has
changed considerably over the past two decades and so have the
performers who make their periodic million starring in high-class
oaters. The likes of John Wayne (who started in program westerns,
won his stardom in drama and then returned to the genre for his
greatest fame), Gary Cooper and James Stewart have been virtually
replaced by the anti-heroes—Lee Marvin, George Kennedy and James
Garner. Kids today are far too cynical to accept the proposition that
good triumphs over evil with the inevitable certainty of the program
western.

But the passage of time and a national binge of nostalgia has
endowed the B western with a respectability that it never knew during
its heyday, while at the same time renewing the luster that once sur-

rounded those tumbleweed troubadours who spent their celluloid careers fighting for something in which they believed. By no means has "Riders of the Range" focused attention on all those who fought on the side of western screen justice during those turbulent years. I have tried to treat the obscure as well as the famous, but as always there seems to be more of the former than of the latter and while their importance may be questionable to some, the story just isn't complete without their mention. The following pages contain a few of those personalities who played but a minor role in the oft-fought battle for the frontier, yet their names linger in the roll call of memory like old friends and here we pay our homage.

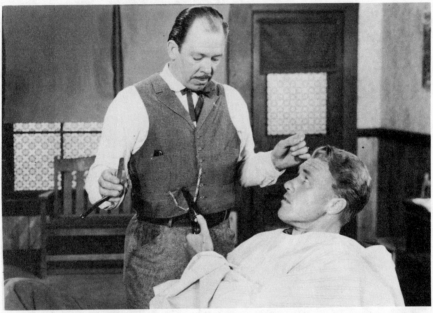

A former sportcaster turned stuntman, Jim Bannon became the fourth actor to portray **Red Ryder** in a 1949-51 series for Eagle-Lion. Bannon came the closest physically to re-creating the comic strip hero as Fred Harmon had created him, but after the Ryder series was finished, he slipped back into stunt work and supporting roles. This is from **Roll, Thunder, Roll** (1949).

This looks like Buffalo Bill, but if you study the stance, it can only be
one man—**The Lone Ranger.** Clayton Moore played many other roles in
his years before the camera, but his career as the masked crime fighter
of the West in movies and on tv overshadowed any of his other work.

Ray "Crash" Corrigan and Bob Livingston, two of the "Three Mes-
quiteers," a popular Republic series that featured numerous actors (including John Wayne) in the leading roles. That pretty lady in Bob's
arms is none other than Rita Hayworth, and the epic is **Hit the Saddle.**

Dick Foran was popular at Universal and Warners. One of the few singing cowboys who could really sing, the versatile performer rose to western popularity in the mid-thirties and was seen on-screen for years in all sorts of roles.

John "Dusty" King, Dave Sharpe and Max Terhune. King's career was brief and Terhune supported several other stars, but Sharpe proved to be more durable. A stuntman second only to Yakima Canutt, he worked as hero, villain, double and eventually became a second unit (action) director.

Jack Luden came to the screen in 1926 with a promising performance in **Fascinating Youth,** then starred in an FBO western series before fading out of sight when sound took over. Luden reappeared in the mid-thirties with a Columbia series of singing westerns. **Pioneer Trail** (1938) starred Jack and Tuffy, and featured Charles Whittaker, Marin Sais and Wally Wales in support.

Jim Newill is best remembered for his **Renfrew of the Royal Mounted** series. When the popular radio character was transferred to the screen in 1937, Newill, a tenor who had worked on the Burns and Allen radio show, was given the lead. **Renfrew** had the makings of a popular western series but slipshod production gave it a low box-office average and Newill went into the **Texas Rangers** series at PRC with Dave O'Brien and Guy Wilkerson before leaving the screen in the mid-forties.

After finishing a series for PRC, Lee Powell (second left) came to fame as **The Lone Ranger** in a 1938 serial of the same name. Leaving a promising career to join the USMC during the war, Powell was killed in action in July 1944 during the invasion of Tinian in the Mariana Islands.

Another country and western singing star of the National Barn Danc[e] Eddie Dean (r) appeared for PRC and Eagle-Lion between 1945-5[0] Dean was not a particularly good actor nor was he even average in t[he] saddle, but his series had two redeeming qualities—it introduced [Al] LaRue to western fans and gave reviewers headaches.